O/N 002144 13.4.88

CLASS No
6.001.5(52)

CW01523019

-7 APR 1988

LIBRARY

Evaluating Applied Research

Report of a Study Commissioned from the
Technical Change Centre by the Assessment Unit,
Research and Technology Policy Division,
Department of Trade and Industry

Evaluating Applied Research: Lessons from Japan

John Irvine

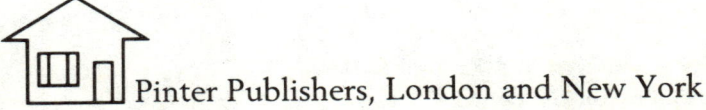
Pinter Publishers, London and New York

© Crown Copyright, 1988

First published in Great Britain in 1988 by
Pinter Publishers Limited
25 Floral Street, London WC2E 9DS

All rights reserved. No part of this publication may be reproduced, stored in a retrieval system, or transmitted by any other means without the prior written permission of the copyright holder. Please direct all enquiries to the publishers.

British Library Cataloguing in Publication Data

A CIP catalogue record for this book is available
from the British Library

ISBN 0-86187-945-7

Library of Congress Cataloging-in-Publication Data

Irvine, John, fl. 1979–
  Evaluating applied research.

  Bibliography: p.
  Includes index.
    1. Research—Japan—Evaluation. 2. Technology—
Research—Japan—Evaluation. 3. Federal aid to
research—Japan.   I. Title.
Q180.J3I77   1988   507'.2052   B7-32746
ISBN 0-86187-945-7

Typeset by Florencetype Ltd, Kewstoke, Avon
Printed by Biddles of Guildford

Contents

List of Figures	vii
Acknowledgements	ix
Foreword (Mr P Hills, Head DTI Assessment Office)	xi
Executive Summary	xii

1. Introduction — 1
   - Background to Study — 1
   - Outline of Study — 1

2. Recent Developments in R&D Evaluation — 8
   - Policy Context — 8
   - Administrative Inspection Bureau — 12
   - Committee on Guidelines for Research Evaluation — 20

3. Evaluation of Applied Research in MITI Agency of Industrial Science and Technology (AIST) — 34
   - Structure and Organization of AIST — 34
   - Basic Technology for Future Industries Programme — 34
   - Large-Scale R&D Programme — 44
   - AIST Laboratories — 50

4. Evaluation of Applied Research by Science and Technology Agency — 58
   - Structure and Organization of STA — 58
   - Special Co-ordination Funds for Science and Technology — 61
   - Exploratory Research for Advanced Technology Programme (ERATO) — 63
   - Research Institutes Administered by STA — 68

5. Evaluation of Applied Research by Companies	73
General Approach to Research Evaluation	73
Evaluation of Government-Funded Research	78
Views on Research Evaluation Within Government	80
6. Conclusions	83
Main Features of Japanese Evaluation System	83
Evaluation Methods and Techniques Employed	85
Lessons from Japan	88
References	92
Appendix 1 List of Officials Consulted	96
Appendix 2 Sample Questionnaire for Visit to Science and Technology Agency Affiliated Laboratories	98
Index	101

List of Figures and Tables

Figures

1	Organizational structure of Japanese research system	5
2	Organization of government in Japan	13
3	Recommended evaluation procedure in national laboratories	26
4	Research classification scheme employed by Council for Science and Technology	28
5	Organization of Agency of Industrial Science and Technology	35
6	Budget and personnel of Agency of Industrial Science and Technology, fiscal year 1986	36
7	Technical targets achieved in Jisedai Project and results obtained in designed alloys	40
8	Summary of research activities of AIST institutes	51
9	Outline of Exploratory Research for Advanced Technology Programme (ERATO)	65

Tables

1	Points and items commonly applied to the Administrative Inspection Bureau Survey of Experimental and Research Organizations	16
2	Organizational participation in Basic Technology for Future Industries Programme	37

3	Goals and candidate technical approaches in 3-D Project	43
4	AIST Large-Scale R&D Programme — ongoing projects	45
5	AIST Large-Scale R&D Programmes — completed projects	46
6	Research activities and budget of Science and Technology Agency, fiscal year 1985	59
7	Evaluation methods and techniques used to assess applied research in Japan	86

Acknowledgements

This report presents the findings of a five-week study on the evaluation of applied research in Japan commissioned from the Technical Change Centre by the Assessment Unit, Research and Technology Policy Division, Department of Trade and Industry. The author would like to express his gratitude to the many officials in Japanese government agencies, research institutes and companies who gave up their time to be consulted in the course of the study. Particular thanks go to Professors F Kodama and M Tanaka (Saitama University) who explained in detail the procedures employed to evaluate R & D in Japan, to Dr C Bradley and Ms Y Otsuka (British Embassy, Tokyo) for providing extremely valuable background guidance and arranging the programme of visits, to Miss Y Ofuji and Miss M Watanabe who acted as interpreters, to Mr B Avery and Mr E Davis (Department of Trade and Industry) and Dr Y Baba, Professor C Freeman and Mr B Martin (SPRU) for constructive criticism of an earlier draft of this report, and to Miss S Powell and Ms C A Gaterell for secretarial assistance.

Despite the central importance of Japan in the world R & D arena, there is still very little English-language material available on how its research system operates. It was for this reason, as well as the widespread current interest in R & D evaluation, that the decision was taken to publish this report to DTI in book form. The intention is that it will go some way to informing researchers, research managers and policy-makers about Japanese approaches to evaluating applied research, and hopefully to stimulating debate about the extent to which we in the West can learn from the methods and techniques they employ. That said, the short-term nature of the study does mean that the report should be regarded as no more than an overview of the Japanese evaluation system. Moreover, despite attempts to check the accuracy of the source material (much of which came from interviews conducted through interpreters), it is probably inevitable that some errors and misinterpretations will remain.

Acknowledgements

Finally, it should be stressed that the findings of this report are the responsibility of the author alone, and do not necessarily reflect the views of the Department of Trade and Industry or the Technical Change Centre.

Foreword

I am glad to have this opportunity to introduce the report which John Irvine has written on the Japanese approach to evaluating applied research.

All over the world there is increasing recognition of the important role evaluation can and must play in ensuring that maximum benefit is gained from the resources invested in research. This imperative applies to the Department of Trade and Industry as much as any. In 1985/86 we spent £185.8m supporting applied research at our own research establishments and in industry. This was 50.5% of our total R&D budget and the UK needs to make the most effective use of this investment.

In commissioning the report, the Department of Trade and Industry's R&D Assessment Unit hopes to learn about, and make a contribution to, a developing methodology. I believe that in the event we shall do both.

Philip Hills
Assessment Unit/Research & Technology Policy Division
Department of Trade and Industry

Executive Summary

1. This report presents the findings of a study aiming to establish what experience exists in Japan with the evaluation of government-funded applied research, and whether any lessons can be drawn for the use of assessment techniques in the UK.

2. Over twenty Japanese organizations responsible for commissioning or conducting evaluation of research were visited. They included national agencies undertaking inter-departmental co-ordination and management of research; government departments and funding agencies which support research intended to find application in an industrial context; academics, consultants and other experts with experience in R&D evaluation; and a number of research institutes and technology-based firms.

3. The questions addressed focused on the methods and techniques employed for evaluating applied research; the extent to which they are used for routine monitoring, mid-term and ex-post evaluation; the strengths and weaknesses of different approaches to evaluation; the objectives of assessment activities; details relating to the planning, organization and timing of evaluation; and allocation of responsibility for overseeing and executing assessment activities.

4. The report shows that the Japanese government has over recent years begun to place greater emphasis on achieving 'value-for-money' in its expenditure on research. This has led to an increase in central government activities in R&D evaluation. Of special note are the evaluation procedures being developed by the Administrative Inspection Bureau (AIB), which as part of its overall remit of improving the efficiency of state organizations has been charged with reviewing the activities of all government laboratories and public research corporations. Assessment is undertaken not only of the value of research output and whether adequate in-house mechanisms are in place for monitoring and evaluation, but attention is most importantly directed

on the continuing 'mission relevance' of institutes. 'Hearings' conducted with industry are a significant feature of the evaluation process. This is the first time that systematic external review has been undertaken of the activities of Japanese government laboratories. It is recommended that consideration be given to studying in detail the AIB approach to research assessment to determine its applicability for evaluating laboratories in the UK.

5. Also noteworthy is a parallel initiative of the Council for Science and Technology (CST) to set up a 'Committee on Guidelines for Research Evaluation'. This aims to promote the introduction of techniques for formal assessment of R&D within government programmes and laboratories, and has produced a set of specifications for effective evaluation together with recommended procedures for monitoring and assessing research performance. These could have relevance outside the purely Japanese context and would therefore repay further study, as would a set of background reports on research evaluation commissioned by the Science and Technology Agency from the Asahi Research Centre. It is too early to evaluate the impact of the CST initiative, but both the Council and the Science and Technology Agency have begun to implement the evaluation guidelines in their own research programmes. Some resistance is, however, being met, particularly from large laboratories funded by other agencies. It is recommended that the published reports of the Committee should be translated into English.

6. Although differences exist across funding agencies and programmes, a few key features characterize the general Japanese approach to assessing government-funded applied research:
(a) The procedures for project selection, management of research, and review of performance have traditionally been closely integrated. This is a function of the reliance on consensus-based committee structures in all parts of the R&D system, and results in the rapid implementation of the results of evaluations;
(b) Great stress is invariably placed on ex-ante evaluation coupled with relatively informal routine monitoring of research progress, with decisions on continuation of funding being made during the annual round of budgetary discussions. The role of the agency officials managing programmes is extremely important in this process;
(c) In recent years, routine monitoring has increasingly been complemented by more formal mid-term and ex-post evaluation,

often using external assessment committees appointed for the lifetime of a programme or project. As yet, peer-review of the type common in Western nations is rarely employed. The use of mid-term reviews, especially in longer-term projects, enables research goals to be revised in the light of changes in technology or the commercial environment;

(d) Significant emphasis is placed in evaluation on the extent to which detailed technical targets have been realized. Targets are normally agreed after lengthy consensus-seeking discussions between companies, laboratories and funding agencies. The fact that research is initiated in the context of agreed strategic industrial and technological objectives means that it is generally accepted that evaluation can often be limited to appraisal of technical performance;

(e) Widespread use is made of publications and patents as indicators of research output and ·technological excellence, especially in relation to the contributions made by institutes to longer-term government-funded research projects carried out jointly with industry. Citation analysis is undertaken only rarely. Government does not see it as necessary or feasible to estimate the rate-of-return on its investment in R&D, preferring to evaluate research in terms of whether national strategic technological aims have been achieved;

(f) It is accepted practice in major applied research programmes to build evaluation into projects even before they begin, and not to add it on at the end for purely auditing purposes as often happens in the UK. This is because evaluation is regarded as an integral part of the research management system.

7. As regards evaluation of collaborative government–industry projects, the current best practice in Japan seems to lie in the approach employed by the Agency of Industrial Science and Technology to assess the Basic Technology for Future Industries Programme. Industry and research institutes both judge the procedures for project definition and selection, routine monitoring, mid-term and final assessment to be working well. The use of independent assessment committees and external peer-review was also welcomed, with firms accepting that the reliance on experts drawn from universities and institutes (rather than from industry) helps protect the commercial interests of company participants.

8. There is little to be learnt from Japanese experience with in-

house evaluation of government laboratories, apart from noting the similarity of many of the problems they face with those of their counterparts in the UK. There may be merit, however, in giving consideration to the potential utility of the detailed forms employed for monitoring individual projects and staff. These elicit a great deal of output information and provide the basis, should it be required, for more systematic internal assessment of research than is currently conducted.

9. The procedures used by companies for evaluating research are generally more systematic than those employed within government. Stress is placed on setting technical goals and regularly monitoring whether pre-established 'milestones' are being achieved. Analyses of technology transfer and commercial benefits are key components in evaluation, but other factors are also considered. Use is made of publications and patents in assessment, especially in relation to longer-term research where the technological impacts are diffuse and the economic returns therefore difficult to predict. The companies interviewed all felt it important to estimate the rates-of-return on research investments, although their inaccuracy was regarded as problematic. Since firms themselves have in practice to pay a significant proportion of the costs of participating in government-funded projects, the approach to assessment employed is generally similar to that of other company-funded longer-term research. Neither companies nor government agencies regarded the criterion of 'additionality' employed by the Department of Trade and Industry as a useful means of evaluating the success of industrial applied research supported by public funds.

10. Companies overall were reasonably satisfied with the way in which government agencies evaluate their collaborative research programmes. They regarded the recent introduction of systematic mid-term assessment and more independent review committees as major improvements on previous practice. Given the participation of industry in programme definition and management, the emphasis in evaluation on comparing technical outcomes with planned targets was felt to be correct. In contrast, companies expressed dissatisfaction with the level and nature of agency evaluation of their own institutes. The quality of research undertaken was regarded as uneven, with some laboratories having problems with ageing staff and renewing old lines of work. They felt that greater use needs to be made of external review in which industry should play a central role.

xvi *Executive Summary*

11. More generally, although the trend to increased assessment of government-funded research was widely welcomed, several problems were identified by those interviewed. First, external assessment is culturally somewhat alien to the Japanese research community because of the traditional reliance on internal consensus-based mechanisms for managing R&D. Consequently it is likely to be resisted if imposed from above. Thought therefore needs to be given to the process for introducing formal evaluation systems if they are to operate satisfactorily. Second, creativity can be impaired if evaluation is undertaken too mechanistically (researchers may, for example, maximize their performance in terms of specified output indicators to the detriment of innovative work). Third, undue pressure to demonstrate immediate technological outputs may stifle longer-term research where the commercial impact is often diffuse and unpredictable, and only becomes evident several years after its completion. The timing of post-hoc evaluation therefore needs to take into account the nature of the research being assessed. Fourth, there is a temptation for government to adopt evaluation techniques which lend themselves to simple quantification—for example, while rate-of-return techniques may be appropriate for individual companies, they were overwhelmingly felt to be unsuitable for use by government. Last, the commercial significance of many joint industry–institute research programmes means that the issue of industrial involvement in both project selection and evaluation is sometimes problematic and needs to be handled sensitively.

12. Finally, while there is much to be learned from the Japanese approach to R&D evaluation, it needs to be recognized that countries like the UK are currently facing a slightly different set of problems in restructuring their research systems to meet the technological needs of the next decade. The Japanese have developed a highly effective system for planning, managing and evaluating research intended to make incremental contributions to science and technology. Their major aim now is to overcome some of the inherent conservative tendencies of this system in order to develop a more appropriate environment for achieving similar levels of success in creative longer-term research. In many respects, the UK faces exactly the opposite problem, which makes the lessons that can be drawn from previous Japanese experience all the more valuable.

1
Introduction

Background to Study

In recent years, concern has grown in most industrialized nations about the need to obtain 'value for money' from public expenditure on research. While there is now a large published literature and a developing consensus on 'best practice' in the evaluation of more basic research,[1] this is not yet the case with research of a strategic or applied nature.[2] Probably the main reason is that assessment of applied research tends to be carried out either in mission-oriented government agencies or in firms, with the result that far less on the subject finds its way into journal articles and published reports. This problem is especially significant in the case of Japan where the language barrier further adds to the difficulty of obtaining information on the approaches to evaluation employed in the wide range of government-funded applied research programmes. This report presents the findings of a five-week study commissioned by the British Department of Trade and Industry which aimed to establish exactly what experience exists in Japan with the assessment of applied research, and whether any lessons might be drawn for the use of evaluation methods and techniques in the UK.[3]

Outline of Study

The complex and often confidential nature of the subject under study meant that information had to be collected mainly through in-depth interviews with those organizations in Japan which commission or undertake evaluation of research. A two-week programme of visits was made to national agencies reponsible for inter-departmental co-ordination and management of research; government departments, funding agencies and laboratories which support or carry out research intended to find subsequent application in an industrial and manufacturing context (we were not concerned with research in agriculture, health or the environment); academics, consultants and other experts with experience in R&D evaluation; and a number of large technology-based firms spanning the electronic and electrical engineering, chemical and biotechnology sectors.

The first step in the study was to carry out a brief scan of the literature on the evaluation of applied research, this being defined as:

original investigation undertaken in order to acquire new knowledge which is directed towards practical aims or objectives. Some applied research is *strategic* where practical applications are likely and feasible but cannot yet be clearly specified. *Specific* applied research has as its aim a quite specific and detailed product, process, system, etc. [emphasis added].[4]

An interview questionnaire was then prepared (employing slightly different questions for companies and governmental agencies) which aimed to address the main practical and technical problems normally involved in evaluating applied research (a sample questionnaire used for Science and Technology Agency laboratories is attached as Appendix 2). These were:

(i) What methods and techniques are used for (a) routine monitoring, and (b) evaluating ex-post the success of applied research?
(ii) To what extent have such methods and techniques been used (routinely or experimentally) by government departments, research-funding agencies and industrial firms?
(iii) What has been the experience with using particular evaluation techniques: what strengths and weaknesses have been identified in their application?
(iv) Does the use of such techniques generally add significantly to the information available when research is initiated and, if so, at what stage?
(v) Are any of these techniques especially suitable for assessing the impact of government-supported applied research (in contrast, for example, to their suitability for evaluating the R&D funded within companies)?

In addressing these main issues, several more detailed points were also covered, wherever possible by reference to specific case studies:

(vi) What has been the main aim behind evaluations of applied research (for example, to provide background information for future funding

decisions, to assess the extent to which the work has contributed to technical progress, or to evaluate the performance of researchers)?
(vii) Has it generally proved helpful to require verifiable detailed evaluation objectives for applied research before it is undertaken?
(viii) At what stage in an applied research (or follow-on) programme is evaluation most often conducted? Are specific evaluation plans agreed at a preliminary stage of programme formulation, or devised and tacked on later as necessary?
(ix) Who initiates evaluation of applied research and what happens to completed studies? Who carries out such evaluations? What knowledge and skills are needed? What relationship is there between evaluators, the funding body and the researchers?

In order to draw general conclusions about the potential utility of different approaches to research evaluation employed in Japan, it was necessary to visit a variety of organizations. These were as follows:

(i) Prime Minister's Office
    Administrative Inspection Bureau, Management and Co-ordination Agency
    Council for Science and Technology
(ii) Agency of Industrial Science and Technology, Ministry of International Trade and Industry
    Technology Research and Information Division
    Office for Large-Scale R&D Projects
    Office for R&D of Basic Technology for Future Industries
    Electrotechnical Laboratory
    Mechanical Engineering Laboratory
    National Chemical Laboratory for Industry
    National Research Laboratory of Metrology
(iii) Science and Technology Agency
    Science and Technology Policy Bureau
    National Institute for Research in Inorganic Materials
    National Research Institute for Metals
(iv) Public corporations
    Institute of Physical and Chemical Research
    Japan Information Centre for Science and Technology
    Research Development Corporation of Japan (Programme for Exploratory Research for Advanced Technology – ERATO)
(v) Industrial and consultancy companies
    Hitachi Ltd.

Introduction

       Mitsubishi Electric Corporation
       NEC Corporation
       Nomura Research Institute
       Sharp Corporation
       Toray Industries
(vi) Universities
       Saitama University (Graduate School for Policy Science).

Figure 1 situates the roles of the various government agencies and laboratories in the context of the overall Japanese research system. Taken together, the organizations visited, especially the AIST and STA laboratories, undertake a range of applied research similar in nature to that supported by the UK Department of Trade and Industry (DTI). The choice of organizations to be covered in the study was made in consultation with the DTI Assessment Unit. A list of the officials interviewed is given in Appendix 1.

In what follows, Chapter 2 first examines recent developments in R&D evaluation in Japan, focusing on the work of the Administrative Inspection Bureau and the Council for Science and Technology Committee on Guidelines for Research Evaluation. Chapter 3 reviews evaluation procedures in programmes and laboratories supported by the Agency of Industrial Science and Technology, while Chapter 4 deals with those financed by the Science and Technology Agency. Chapter 5 discusses the procedures and techniques used by companies to evaluate their strategic and applied research programmes, especially those which are government funded and carried out in collaboration with AIST or STA laboratories. Finally, in Chapter 6 the main features of the Japanese approach to evaluating government-funded applied research are identified. An attempt is also made to identify lessons which can usefully be learned for improving evaluation practice in the UK. Given the time contraints on the study, the report aims to be descriptive and synthetic but not prescriptive.

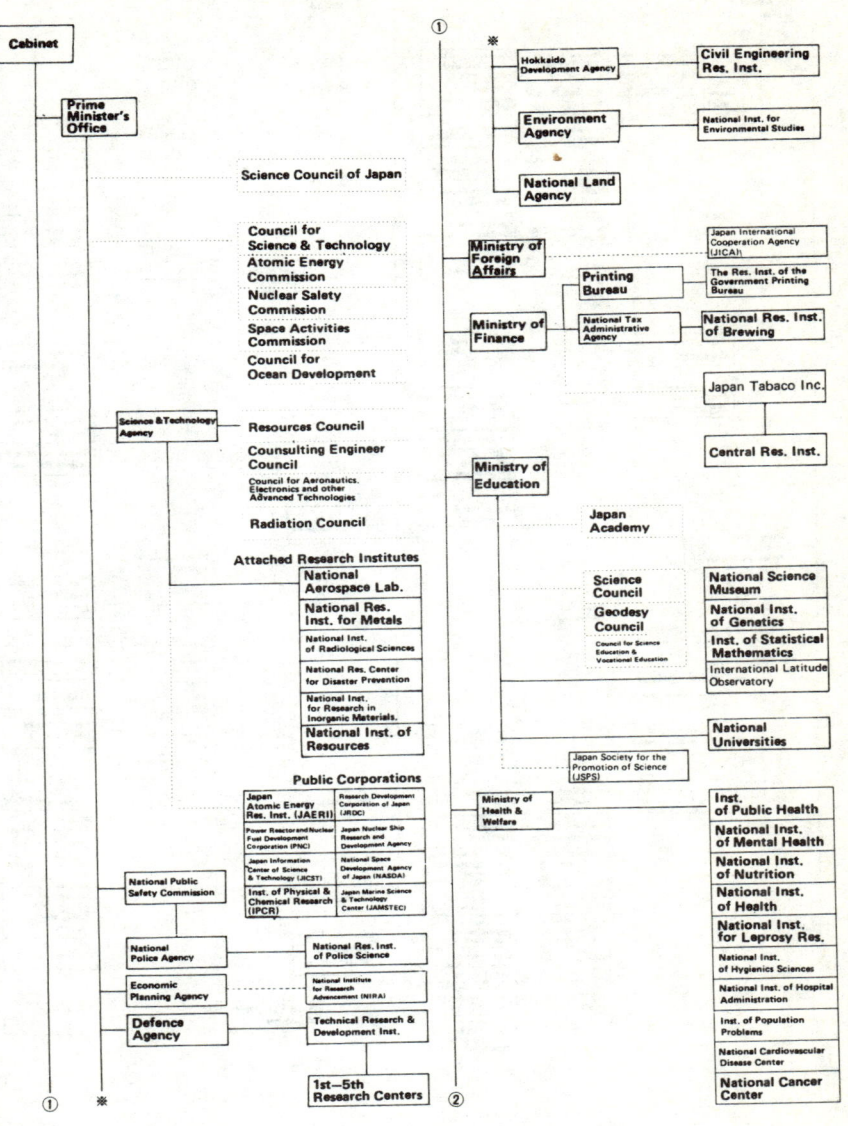

Figure 1 Organizational structure of Japanese research system
Source: Science and Technology Agency (1985b, pp. 30–1)

6 Introduction

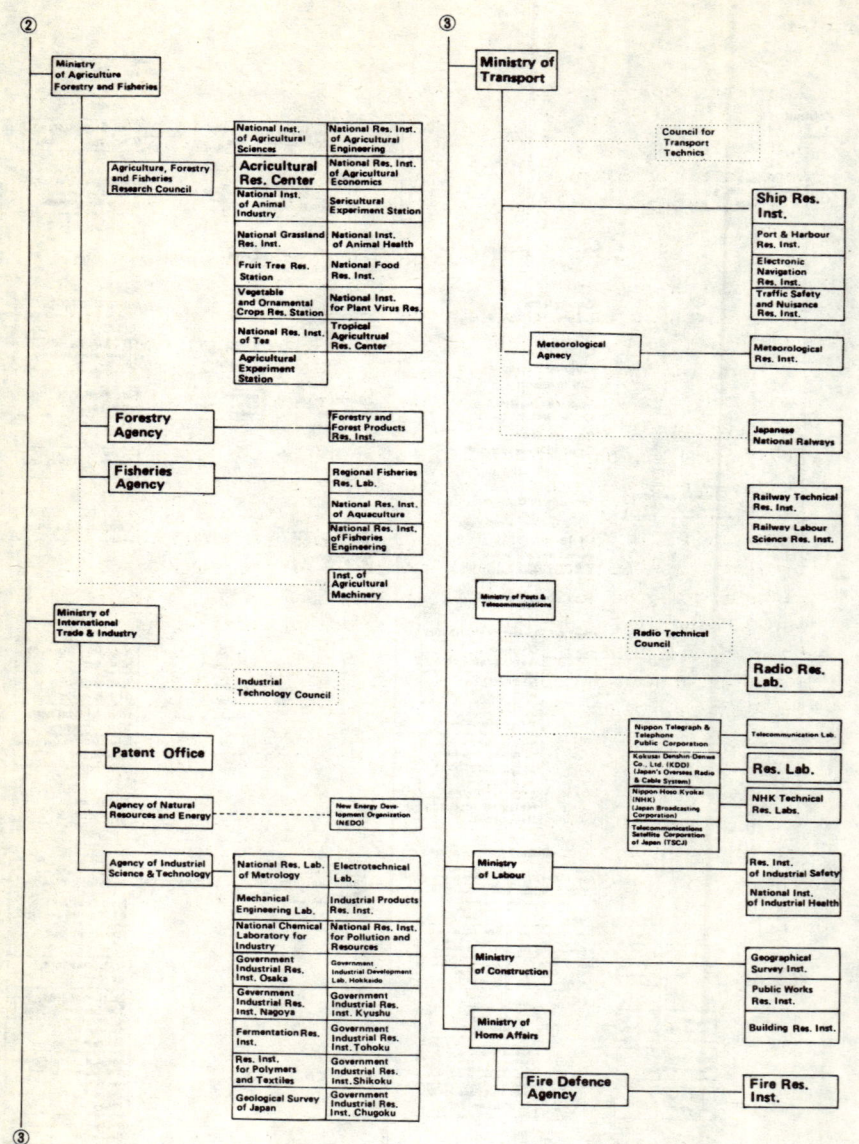

Figure 1 – *cont.*
Source: Science and Technology Agency (1985b, pp. 30–1)

Notes

1. See, for example, Luukkonen-Gronow (1987), OECD (1987), Office of Technology Assessment (1986), Logsdon and Rubin (1985), and Irvine and Martin (1985).
2. One important exception is a recent initiative by NORDFORSK, the Nordic Co-operative Organization for Applied Research—see Ormala (1987).
3. Studies on evaluation practice in a number of other industrial nations have also been commissioned by DTI from PREST, University of Manchester. The results are reported in Gibbons and Georghiou (1987).
4. This is the definition of 'applied research' employed by the Department of Trade and Industry, and is based on that used in British official statistics (see Cabinet Office, 1986, Annex 3, p. 183). Other definitions are in widespread use elsewhere—see, for example, Irvine and Martin (1984, p. 4). In Japan, the official definition of applied research is 'research undertaken primarily for the advancement of scientific knowledge, with a specific practical application sought directly' (Statistics Bureau, 1987, p. 204). However, much of what would commonly be regarded as applied research is often referred to as basic research (see, for example, Frieman, 1987, p. 4–11). As a result, 'strategic research' is normally included under the category of basic research while applied research covers the British category of 'specific applied research' plus a certain amount of development activities. As in many other countries, the Japanese recognize the need for improved definitions—the Council for Science and Technology, for example, has recently made use of complex four-fold research classification scheme: (a) basic applied research; (b) non-basic applied research; (c) basic non-applied research; and (d) non-basic non-applied research. This is outlined in Chapter 2 (see also Council for Science and Technology 1986b, p. 4). Strategic research is primarily included under category (a).

2
Recent Developments in R & D Evaluation

Policy Context

As in other industrial countries, R&D evaluation has now become an important policy issue for the Japanese government. The need for improved evaluation procedures for both basic and applied research was highlighted by the 1984 Report on the 11th Inquiry of the Council for Science and Technology (CST), an advisory body attached to the Prime Minister's Office with the role of formulating long-term national policy goals for R&D.[1] It is worth quoting the relevant section of the report in its entirety.

It has become increasingly essential to conduct rational evaluation of research in order to promote R&D more effectively under restricted time and limited R&D resources, especially with regard to R&D promoted by the government. It is important that the evaluation is done from the point of view of an objective observer and with the intention of promoting the creativity of the researchers concerned. At the same time, the evaluation of research should be undertaken in accordance with the character of the research, its stage of progress, its conditions, etc. In other words, in the case of basic or fundamental research, importance should be attached to creativity and the evaluation should be done from a long-range point of view. In this case, evaluation of the methods of research should be undertaken in such a way as to enable the researchers to make the most of their creativity and independence, and evaluation of the results should be based on mutual evaluation among the researchers themselves (i.e. peer review), their long-range effects and their academic impact. In the case of applied or developmental research, it is more effective to evaluate the methods and research objectives beforehand and to promote such research systematically. This is because what is important here is to develop the results of research into practical technology effectively and efficiently, based on existing basic knowledge and economic or social needs. As for R&D which extends over a long period, it is essential to make interim assessments at certain intervals so as to review the research objectives and plan from time to time in line with the progress of research and with changes in the external environment. Furthermore, upon conclusion of each research programme, it is necessary to assess how far the original objectives have been achieved and, at the same time, to make positive use of the results of the research including those cases where the original objectives have not yet been achieved.

R&D evaluation should be strengthened primarily at the organs which are in charge of carrying out the R&D activities. In such cases, it is necessary also to improve and prepare the organizations and conditions for evaluation in accord with the nature of the R&D concerned by, for example, including a third party to improve the evaluation system. ... On the part of the administrative organs concerned, it is necessary for them to conduct adequate surveys and analysis beforehand with regard to the progress of R&D and changes in the surrounding environment when they prepare their plans and guidelines relating to the respective fields for which they are responsible. ... At the same time, it is essential for them to clarify their R&D plans and decide on priorities, and improve their evaluation of research [CST, 1984, pp. 18–19, English translation slightly revised from original].

There are six main reasons underlying this increased interest in R&D evaluation in Japan. First, a central element in the political programme of the Nakasone administration has been to improve the effectiveness with which government funds are spent, a priority stemming from the need to put a brake on the growth of the large public sector deficit. As in the UK, agencies funding R&D are now having to demonstrate greater accountability and value for money in their spending on research programmes and laboratories.

Second, the rapid expansion in government-funded research during the 1970s[2] has since given way to a period of more modest growth. Coupled with the escalating demands being placed by industry on the state-funded R&D infrastructure, this has led to a reappraisal of how research funds should most effectively be allocated and spent. Evaluation is seen as playing a major role in all aspects of R&D management spanning preassessment, ongoing monitoring of research, mid-term assessment and ex-post evaluation.

Third, and of central importance, has been the marked improvement in Japan's international scientific and technological position over recent years. The country has changed from being a 'technological follower' to a 'technological leader' with the result that it is no longer possible in many fields merely to emulate a 'working textbook' established in North America and Europe (Yamauchi, 1983). While success in programmes to 'catch up with the West' could be measured in terms of whether the results matched or improved upon foreign work, the criteria are now rather less clear. This leads to a problem in that laboratories and researchers will increasingly be

> entering fields heretofore unexplored where no information that could be used as reference material is available. In a situation such as this, the researcher must be aware of how best to carry out his research, and based on his own judgement, must confirm the direction or course of that research. A research evaluation system could prove an essential means of making sure of the course of one's research, i.e. that one is on the right track and proceeding in the direction that is most likely to yield the sought after results. If research evaluation is not gradually implemented and the direction and course adjustments of research programmes are not carried out based on these evaluations, then any real improvements in research and development efficiency will fail to materialize.
> One factor that has to be given due consideration when we speak of research into previously unexplored domains is the increased risk involved in such research. Hedges against big risks will have to be built into the management systems of these kinds of research. It will be necessary to develop a system that affords the researcher the chance to challenge risky endeavours free from worry. In other words, it is essential to put together a system that takes the risks of both management and researcher into consideration. The establishment of a research evaluation system would serve as the core of such a system [Kodama et al., 1981, pp. 2–3].[3]

Fourth, the oscillating price of energy and raw materials (upon which Japan is so dependent) has in some cases resulted in failure to implement costly technologies developed in the long-term AIST 'sunshine' (new energy technologies) and 'moonlight' (energy conservation technologies) programmes and in certain STA energy programmes (for example, nuclear ship propulsion). This has happened despite achieving the technical goals set in the R&D planning stage, and it has focused attention on the need for more thorough and periodic stage assessment of research programmes to ascertain whether the anticipated results continue to be of potential economic or technological value.

Fifth, there has been a significant change in the research function specified by government for the large mission-oriented laboratories operated by AIST and STA. While the growth of strong industrial laboratories in the post-war period had already forced most institutes away from their former role of providing central support and facilities to companies for application-oriented R&D, they remained until recently (and in some cases still are) heavily involved in specific applied research. In contrast, their prime mission for the future as laid out in the 1985 'White Paper on Science and Technology' is to concentrate on 'object-oriented basic work' (i.e. strategic research) and 'creative basic technology' (STA, 1985a). Although some institutes (for example, the Electrotechnical Laboratory) are already well equipped for this role, others still require substantial restructuring, in particular to phase out old lines of work. Evaluation will be important both in assessing whether current programmes are in line with national needs and whether research is being executed and disseminated effectively. This problem is compounded by an ageing problem among researcheres (the average age of professional staff in national laboratories is around 43) which will be difficult to solve because of the system of lifetime employment for government officials. One solution has been gradually to transfer research funds away from core support ('normal research') to collaborative programme grants ('designated research') which are more closely evaluated.

Finally, there has been a growing awareness that the traditional consensus-based committee structures employed to plan and manage research are not always wholly appropriate for making decisions in which major changes in direction are necessary—for example, to terminate the operation of an institute or end prematurely a large research programme because of poor performance. The situation is well summarized by Tanaka (1987, pp. 9–10):

The problems of this consensus-making system related to evaluation ... are two-fold. One is that it takes time for a number of people to discuss and agree the conclusions ... A more important problem is that [such a] system does not function well in cases where the subject is extremely serious and complicated. If the case is, for example, to abolish an R&D programme or to stop a project in the course of construction, there might remain little room for compromise. Government departments may, necessarily, defend their ongoing policies and it may become difficult to draw final conclusions. In other words, the consensus-making system for evaluation might work well for incremental improvements or creating a new type of R&D programme because there is little pain among the parties concerned. As a matter of fact, there have been few examples of R&D programmes being abolished and ongoing projects being stopped in response to the findings of committees. On the other hand, there are many examples of programmes being improved or new programmes being created [English slightly revised from original].

Recognition of the importance of these problems has influenced the assessment approach developed by the Administrative Inspection Bureau for reviewing national laboratories, and the framework and guidelines for R&D evaluation established in 1986 by the Council for

Science and Technology. It is worth describing both evaluation initiatives in detail.

Administrative Inspection Bureau

Overall Remit

The Administrative Inspection Bureau (AIB) is part of the Management and Coordination Agency (MCA) which is an 'external organ' of the Prime Minister's Office (see Figure 2). The MCA was established in 1984 with the remit of 'providing the national government with a new structure for vigorous and effective management to ensure that government operations are efficient, well-coordinated and responsive to social and economic change' (MCA 1985, p. 1). The AIB has 150 staff in its Tokyo headquarters (with a further 1000 in local branch offices). These are organized into ten divisions, each headed by an 'inspector'. Seven divisions are responsible for specific ministries and three for interdepartmental activities (for example, 'public corporations'). The official role of AIB is to 'investigate the actual operations of government agencies to analyze and evaluate programmes, and, on the basis of facts or evidence gained through investigation, to make recommendations to the agencies concerned and thus to contribute to the improvement of governmental operations' (ibid., p. 16). Although the AIB has no direct organizational equivalent in the UK, some of its activities are similar to those conducted by the Cabinet Office/Treasury Joint Management Unit, the National Audit Office and the Cabinet Office Science and Technology Assessment Office.

The scope of investigation is broad, covering not just governmental organizations but all publicly-funded programmes. The areas examined include the legality of operation of government agencies, as well as whether 'the objectives are fully achieved and whether or not the efficiency, effectiveness and adequacy of various programmes are maintained' (ibid., p. 16). The results of inspections are normally compiled into reports which make recommendations to the agencies and organizations concerned. These are published after opportunity has been given for internal comment and revision. In cases where improvements are recommended and the subsequent response is judged unsatisfactory by the Bureau, it is formally possible for a further round of inspection to be carried out. However, this is highly unlikely insofar as there is generally a high degree of cooperation

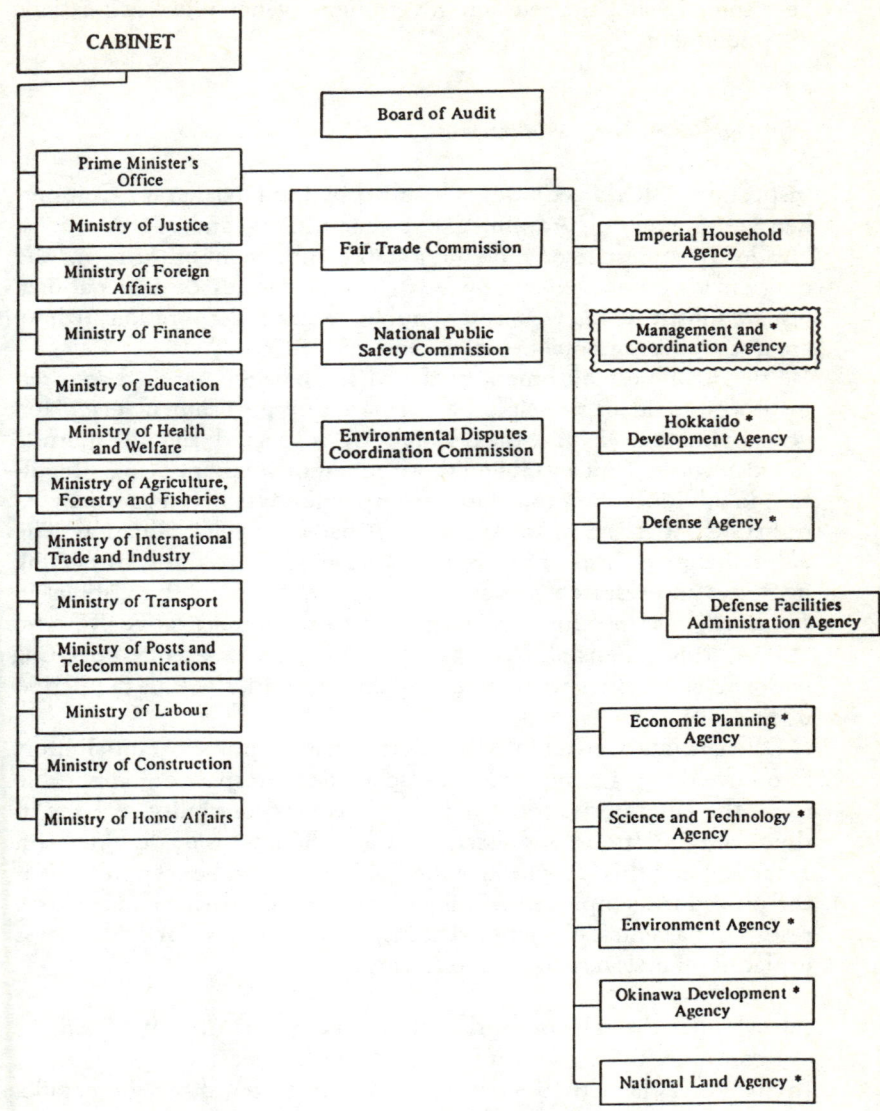

Figure 2 Organization of government in Japan
Source: Management and Coordination Agency (1985, p. 36).
* External organ of the Prime Minister's Office headed by a Minister of State.

between AIB and the relevant government agency when inspections are undertaken.[4]

Inspection of Research Activities

Inspection of R&D activities is handled by the Division for Comprehensive Survey of Administrative Institutions and Corporations. Headed by an inspector and with a staff complement of thirteen,[5] the division is responsible for reviewing the activities of 140 national research institutes as well as ten 'public research corporations' (these are quasi-governmental organizations).

Prior to the establishment of the MCA in 1984, national research institutes could in principle be evaluated by government every ten years. However, by no means all were inspected and the normal practice was to concentrate on those apparently experiencing difficulties. In addition, the procedure for inspection was neither formalized nor systematic, and in some cases was based on self-evaluation. The Administrative Inspection Bureau's responsibilities for inspecting institutes and research corporations were set down by the Cabinet in January 1984 in 'Current Framework for Administrative Reform' (MCA, 1984). This also charged each ministry or agency operating national laboratories with reviewing their activities within the period up to 1989.

Officials interviewed in AIB reported having put substantial effort into developing a comprehensive 'schedule of inspection' applicable to all the laboratories for which they have responsibility. A copy of the main questions addressed in the schedule was provided (in Japanese) and this is reproduced in Table 1. As can be seen, review of the procedures employed within laboratories to manage and evaluate research is a central element in the inspection process. Particular stress is placed on investigating the following:

(a) whether the mission of the laboratory and its main programmes continues to be relevant to national R&D needs;
(b) whether the activities complement and do not duplicate parallel research being undertaken in other national institutes, public laboratories and companies;
(c) the extent to which the objectives of research are well specified and adequate mechanisms exist to set priorities for the use of government core-funding ('ordinary research'), and initiate new

lines of work through earmarked programmes and separately budgeted research ('special research');
(d) whether the planning division and senior staff are effectively managing the progress of research; and
(e) whether mid-term and ex-post evaluation is conducted, how well the assessment criteria are specified, and the extent to which evaluation procedures are systematized.

The first step in the procedure for inspecting institutes is to request the director to provide a full set of recent annual reports (which include summaries of research results), planning documents, progress reports on major studies and financial accounts. These are studied closely and a two-day site visit organized during which the director is typically interviewed for three hours. The remainder of the visit is devoted to an 'internal hearing' with senior institute staff, including the officials in charge of planning, budgeting and evaluation. A large amount of other documentation (described below) is also collected during the discussions.

After evaluating the results of the site visit, 'hearings' with external experts or the 'user community' of the laboratory's research are often conducted.[6] The form of such hearings depends on the mission of the laboratory under review, and for Agency of Industrial Science and Technology institutes would normally involve seeking the views of industry on the relevance and value of the research output. Points of detail remaining to be clarified are then discussed with laboratory management and a report compiled, including any recommendations for change. Laboratory management and the funding agency concerned are then given opportunity to comment, after which final revisions are made and the report published.

To date, the Bureau has carried out inspections of the Japan Information Centre for Science and Technology, the Institute of Physical and Chemical Research, the Social Development Research Institute, and several other administrative organizations. A report on this first batch of evaluations was published in December 1986 (MCA, 1986). Inspection of the National Research Laboratory of Metrology was completed in April 1987, with work continuing on a number of other evaluations including the Japan Atomic Energy Research Institute and the National Chemical Laboratory for Industry.[7]

Table 1 Points and items commonly applied to the Administrative Inspection Bureau Survey of Experimental and Research Organizations*

---

1. **Point of Survey**
   (a) To strengthen and revitalize experimental and research activities.
   (b) To rationalize management of other operations (e.g. support activities).
   (c) To reorganize and rationalize research activities and personnel.

2. **Main Items in Survey**
   (a) *Content of research*
   (i) To adjust and rationalize experimental and research activities whose necessity and importance has declined since they were established as a result of economic and social changes.
   (ii) To ensure an efficient division of roles among the various national research organizations as well as public research organizations, and to adjust and rationalize experimental and research activities to take into account the development of work in private laboratories including joint research laboratories and research associations. Here, note should be taken of the basic role of national experimental research organizations as set out by the Administrative Reform Council:
   – experimental and research work should be left to the private sector as much as possible in those fields where they have the capability. The national research organizations should conduct experiments and research essential to meeting priorities set by government;
   – concerning basic research and large-scale experiments and research, the national experimental and research organizations should conduct R&D in themes and fields it is difficult to expect the private sector to undertake.
   Note should also be taken of the division of labour between national and public (prefectural) experimental and research organizations:
   – national experimental and research organizations aim to undertake basic and leading-edge research in special areas meeting national needs;
   – on the other hand, public experimental and research organizations aim to undertake work diffusing and transferring the results of R&D in national laboratories to regions in line with regional requirements, and also to conduct more applied research on subjects characteristic to each region.
   (iii) To examine whether the objectives of research are well specified.
   (iv) To improve the content of research by achieving the aims set for research tasks.

   (b) *Research administration*
   (i) The procedure for selecting research themes (in both ordinary and special research).
   (ii) Administration, planning and monitoring of research progress.
   (iii) Mid-term and post-hoc assessment of the results of research (evaluation methods, clarification of assessment criteria, systematization of evaluation procedures).
   (iv) Utilization of research results.

Table 1 — *cont.*

(c) *Personnel administration*
(i) Employment and administration of research staff.
(ii) Promotion of extensive and diversified exchange of researchers between industry, universities and government research organizations.
(iii) Introduction of flexible research systems by adopting flexible researcher systems and other measures.
(iv) Positive utilization of older researchers.

(d) *Promotion of commissioned research and collaborative research*

(e) *Approach used to consolidate research basis (including activities of supporting divisions)*

(f) *Reorganization and rationalization*
(i) To reorganize and rationalize experimental and research organizations in line with changes in the social and economic environment (including internal institutional reorganization and rationalization).
(ii) Reduction and relocation of researchers and staff in support divisions in line with reorganization and rationalization of research activities.
(iii) To rationalize required staff by commissioning the private sector to undertake 'common administrative works'.

The Administrative Inspection Bureau should take into account the strong public concern about achieving excellence and relevance in the research activities of experimental and research organizations, and make efforts to understand and collect information on their real situation.

---

* This is an unofficial translation made by the British Embassy, Tokyo, which has not been checked by the Administrative Inspection Bureau. The English text has also been subsequently reworded to improve readability and may therefore contain errors.

Case Studies of Inspection

It is useful to discuss briefly two examples of inspection on which a certain amount of information is available. The first concerns the recently published evaluation of the activities of the Institute of Physical and Chemical Research (RIKEN). Here, the interesting feature is that the Administrative Inspection Bureau requested RIKEN to take steps to bring its research activities closer into line with government policy and national needs. In particular, it recommended closure of the laboratory's major programme on agricultural chemistry (MCA, 1986).

According to AIB staff, the main input to this decision was an evaluation of the nature and impact of the results from the programme. This area of research had been initiated in 1959 at a time when most agricultural chemicals were imported and concern existed about their toxicity and environmental impact. Detailed examination of the results from RIKEN's work showed that it had contributed substantially to developing a strong knowledge base in Japan—a study by the Science and Technology Agency found that, in a four-year period examined, Japanese scientists published 180 papers, while the larger West German and US communities produced 190 and 195 respectively. However, companies had rapidly expanded their activities to take advantage of commercial opportunities in synthetic agricultural chemicals with the result that, by the mid-1980s, they accounted for 1,500 of the 1,600 researchers employed in the field in Japan. Evaluation of the practical benefits from RIKEN's work showed that it had led to the commercial development of only two agro-chemicals, while industry had developed around 150 in the same period.

Taken together with the results of a 'hearing' with representatives from the chemical industry, AIB concluded that

(a) The field of agricultural chemistry was now 'mature' in that most of the necessary basic and strategic research has been undertaken. RIKEN had played a useful role here;
(b) Japan had become relatively strong in this field and industry was now well equipped to carry out its own research programmes;
(c) It was not appropriate for RIKEN to continue undertaking very specific applied research. Not only was this no longer part of its mission, but the laboratory was nowhere near as successful as industry in executing such tasks;
(d) RIKEN should instead concentrate on longer-term strategic research on physiological and ecological processes required to meet emerging medical, agricultural and technological needs.[8]

The other case study concerns the National Research Laboratory of Metrology (NRLM). Since the inspection by AIB had at the time of interviewing in February 1987 only reach the site-visit stage, it was too soon to ascertain the likely outcome of the evaluation. The NRLM staff interviewed were instead asked to describe the questions put to them by the AIB inspectors, in particular on the laboratory's research activities and output. These throw more light on the AIB inspection procedure than the formal schedule of questions listed in Table 1 and are therefore worth listing. The main questions asked were as follows:

(a) How are research activities broken down by field and subfield, and by type of research (basic, applied, etc.)?
(b) How were the current research themes selected and on the basis of what criteria?
(c) What procedures are used to plan new research and to monitor whether ongoing research is being executed efficiently?
(d) What procedures and criteria are employed to evaluate mid-term and ex-post the results of research?
(e) What procedures and criteria are employed to evaluate individual researchers?
(f) What are the main stages in the annual planning calendar — does a flow diagram for yearly planning exist?
(g) How are the 'ordinary expenses' (core funds) for the laboratory distributed?
(h) What publications have been produced by the laboratory's researchers, and how are these broken down by type of publication (articles in international journals, official reports, etc.)?
(i) What presentations have been made by laboratory staff to external audiences (e.g. at conferences or companies)?
(j) How does the director-general of the laboratory monitor the progress of research?
(k) What foreign and domestic patents have been filed, which have been accepted, and what royalties have accrued?
(l) What use is made of large-scale research and testing facilities in the laboratory? Who has used these facilities?
(m) Have any projects been terminated in recent years before the planned completion date? If so, why?
(n) Have any researchers left in recent years and, if so, why? How were such researchers replaced?

It should be noted that citation data are not taken into account by AIB. Nor is much stress placed on commissioned research for industry since national laboratories are discouraged by government from working on commercially confidential research for individual companies (see Chapter 3).

The senior NRLM staff interviewed expressed surprise at the extent and detail of questioning by the AIB officials since the previous inspection by government had focused solely on administrative and financial matters. They were, however, able to provide most of the information requested by the Bureau.

Finally, comment should be made on the impact of the AIB initiative on the institute-based research system. While many of those interviewed had insufficient knowledge to offer an informed judgement (this stems from the fact that the results of only one set of evaluations have been published), most others were relatively positive. Industrialists in particular felt that external inspection was an important development in so far as it provides a necessary mechanism for helping redirect the activities of some of the less productive institutes. Nevertheless, despite the activities of the Bureau, AIB staff expressed strong views that the overall level of evaluation carried out in Japanese mission-oriented government laboratories is still too low. One interviewee stated that:

The situation is not satisfactory ... Evaluation of research results by external experts can be very important, but in fact this is very rare at the moment. When evaluations are carried out, laboratory managements tend to select for review the work carried out by researchers with good reputations—this is a particular problem with a system traditionally based on self-evaluation ... Evaluation systems in Japan still have room for improvement.[9]

Committee on Guidelines for Research Evaluation

The second recent initiative to be considered is the Committee on Guidelines for Research Evaluation, set up under the auspices of the Council for Science and Technology (CST). This published two influential reports in 1986 aimed at promoting the wider adoption of a more systematic approach to research assessment *within* government agencies, programmes and laboratories. As such, the CST initiative can be seen as complementary to that of the Administrative Inspection Bureau.

Overview of Committee's Activities

For the reasons outlined earlier in this chapter, the CST had by the early 1980s become aware of the need to initiate increased evaluation of government-funded research. As a result, the Research Evaluation Subcommittee[10] of the Council set up an ad-hoc Committee on Guidelines for Research Evaluation. This is chaired by Dr J Kondo

(President of the Science Council of Japan) and has a membership of seven drawn from the academic community, public corporations and industry.[11]

The work of the Committee has been carried out in three phases. The first involved defining the 'concept of research evaluation' and answering the question 'what is it and how is it undertaken?' A consultancy company, Asahi Research Centre (ARC), had previously been commissioned by STA to carry out a background study which resulted in three reports on (a) current approaches to research evaluation based on results from a survey of national laboratories (ARC, 1982); (b) approaches to evaluation employed overseas and in the domestic private sector (ARC, 1983); and (c) overall conclusions and a proposed framework for the evaluation of national laboratories (ARC, 1984). The findings of the Asahi study formed the basis of the Committees's first report entitled 'Basic View on Research Evaluation' (CST, 1986a).

The next phase focused on establishing acceptable criteria and methods for research assessment, and resulted in a second report on 'Guidelines for Research Evaluation' (CST, 1986b). The final phase had, at the time of interviewing, only just begun and aims to test the research assessment approach developed by applying it to a number of large-scale R&D projects. This may prove controversial and no details were available.

Asahi Report on Research Evaluation in Japan

The main input to the first phase of the CST Committee's task of developing an evaluation framework was the ARC survey of research assessment within Japanese government laboratories. Replies to postal questionnaires were received from 68 institute directors (a 65 per cent response rate) and 353 senior researchers (30 per cent response rate). Although now somewhat dated, the results are still of interest, providing information on both the extent to which evaluation systems are employed in government laboratories, and the perceptions and views of institute management and researchers concerning assessment. The main findings, which are reported in Kodama *et al.* (1981), were as follows:

(a) There was a general lack of understanding among both management and researchers as to what constitutes a 'proper evaluation system'. Although 70 per cent of managers reported that some

form of evaluation system was in place, only 30 per cent of researchers felt this to be the case (ibid., p. 15).
(b) Awareness of the need for research evaluation was, however, widespread not only among managers (nearly all gave positive replies), but also among the researchers who would be subject to assessment (more than 75 per cent in laboratories without evaluation systems agreed that their introduction would be desirable) (ibid., p. 7).
(c) Two-thirds of researchers in institutes with assessment systems felt that evaluation should be made more formal so as to enable them 'to better grasp the progress of their own research and afford excellent opportunities to listen to outside opinions' (ibid., p. 8).
(d) Only 15 per cent of researchers in laboratories with evaluation systems, and 16 per cent in those without, felt that the use of performance evaluations was invalid.
(e) Distribution of research funds in laboratories without evaluation systems was generally related to numbers of staff in operating units. In those with such systems, funding was more closely related to the work being carried out and 'evaluations performed prior to the start of a given research project . . . were carried out with subject selection and the allocation of resources (funds) in mind' (ibid., p. 10). However, there was evidence of a mismatch between decisions on research themes (made at researcher or research group level) and funding (made at the institute level) which was felt likely to limit the introduction of effective evaluation systems (ibid., p. 16).
(f) 82 per cent of researchers from institutes with evaluation systems reported the existence of mid-term assessments of projects, while the figure for laboratories without was 64 per cent. In addition, the latter showed a higher rate of discontinued projects and budgetary or personnel changes. 'This would seem to support the theory that research can be more efficiently carried out via the incorporation of an evaluation system' (ibid., p. 11).
(g) 92 per cent of researchers from laboratories having evaluation systems, compared to 79 per cent from those without, agreed that there was 'sufficient' or 'average' utilization of the results from their work. 'Thus, it would appear from these findings that evaluation systems contribute to the effective utilization of research results' (ibid., p. 11).
(h) Concerning managerial control of research, 51 per cent of respondents in laboratories with evaluation systems reported being

'hampered in their work' by superiors. This was, however, not significantly greater than the figure of 47 per cent for respondents in institutes without evaluation systems (ibid., p. 12). In addition, 95 per cent felt that official restrictions made it difficult to obtain extra personnel or funds for an ongoing project even when positively evaluated at the mid-term stage. The result is that feedback on evaluation to researchers was seen as leading at best to no change and at worse to negative outcomes (ibid., p. 17).

Although the findings of the survey are by no means clear-cut, Asahi Research Centre were able to conclude that:

research evaluation systems are effectively linked to the selection of research subjects, allocation of resources, discontinuation of ineffective projects and better utilization of research findings . . . If research evaluation systems are properly implemented, they should be capable of fulfilling their inherent roles [ibid., p. 13]

They also identified a number of prerequisites for establishing effective research evaluation systems:

(a) 'Both research managers and researchers themselves will have to be fully aware of the need for research evaluation.'
(b) There needs to exist 'a common understanding of just what research evaluation means on the part of managers and researchers alike — i.e. of the purpose and efficacy of evaluation systems'.
(c) 'Researchers will have to accept the systematization of research evaluation.'
(d) 'Research evaluation systems will have to be linked to managerial decision-making processes.'
(e) 'Means of channelling the results of research evaluations back into research activities will have to be set up.'
(f) 'Mechanisms will have to be provided for within the evaluation process to ensure the researchers of the usefulness and worth of such evaluations.'
(g) 'Should research evaluation be put into practice, it will have to be capable of functioning as expected' (ibid., pp. 7 and 14).

Contents of Committee Reports

The basic message of the Asahi survey is that, although difficult to accomplish, the introduction of more systematic research evaluation has significant potential benefits for researchers and management alike. Consequently, it is in the interests of institutes to initiate development of in-house assessment activities.

The problem faced by the CST Committee was how to translate the Asahi findings into practical recommendations for developing new evaluation systems. In particular, it was felt important that commitment to their introduction would need to be obtained from the research community, and this would not be forthcoming if culturally alien Western-type methods (such as external peer-review) were adopted at the outset. Consequently, it was decided that the best policy would be to recommend an approach focusing on what was termed 'gyroscopic evaluation', that is performance indicators enabling researchers and teams to evaluate their own activities dynamically against a changing external R&D environment. This is a major theme of the first report of the CST Committee (CST, 1986a). The report also brings together a range of other material in developing its 'concept of research evaluation' and 'how it should be undertaken'. No English translation yet exists[12] although one can gain some idea of its contents from the chapter headings:

1 Past history
   (a) Previous attitudes to the evaluation of research
   (b) Views of the Committee on the evaluation of research
   (c) Past activities of the Committee in research evaluation

2 The current situation with research evaluation
   (a) The current status of research evaluation in Japan
       Administrative organizations and departmental laboratories
       Nationally established research institutes
       Private companies
   (b) The current status of research evaluation in foreign nations

3 The concept of research evaluation

4 The desirable structure and system of research evaluation
   (a) System of research evaluation
   (b) Structure of research evaluation
   (c) Desirable status of research evaluation

The features seen as desirable in research evaluation systems form the basis of the recommendations made in the second of the Committee's reports (CST, 1986b). A senior STA official who serviced the Committee summarized the main themes of this report as follows:

(a) Research evaluation needs to be carried out at the level of both individual projects and programmes or groups of projects.
(b) Evaluation of research should be 'systematized' (or formalized). The main elements that need to be specified are:
- the purpose of evaluation;
- who should undertake the evaluation;
- objectives and use to be made of the results;
- the period of evaluation;
- evaluation methods to be employed; and
- the evaluation support system (e.g. data bases).
(c) To ensure that evaluation activities encounter a minimum of problems, four conditions need to be met:
- the evaluation system should be effective, i.e. it must be appropriate for its purpose;
- the system must be flexible, e.g. able to handle different kinds of research;
- the assessment criteria and techniques employed should be made clear to researchers, i.e. they should be 'transparent';
- the system should be continuous.

Particular stress is placed on ensuring that mid-term and ex-post evaluation are related to ex-ante assessment, as is shown in Figure 3 which outlines a recommended procedure for evaluation in government-funded research institutes.

No English translation exists of this second report, so it is again worth listing its contents:

1 Preliminary guidelines for research evaluation
2 Clarification of the nature of research evaluation
   (a) Different views on the evaluation of research
   (b) The Committee's views on the priorities for research evaluation
   (c) The need to take into account the specific characteristics of research

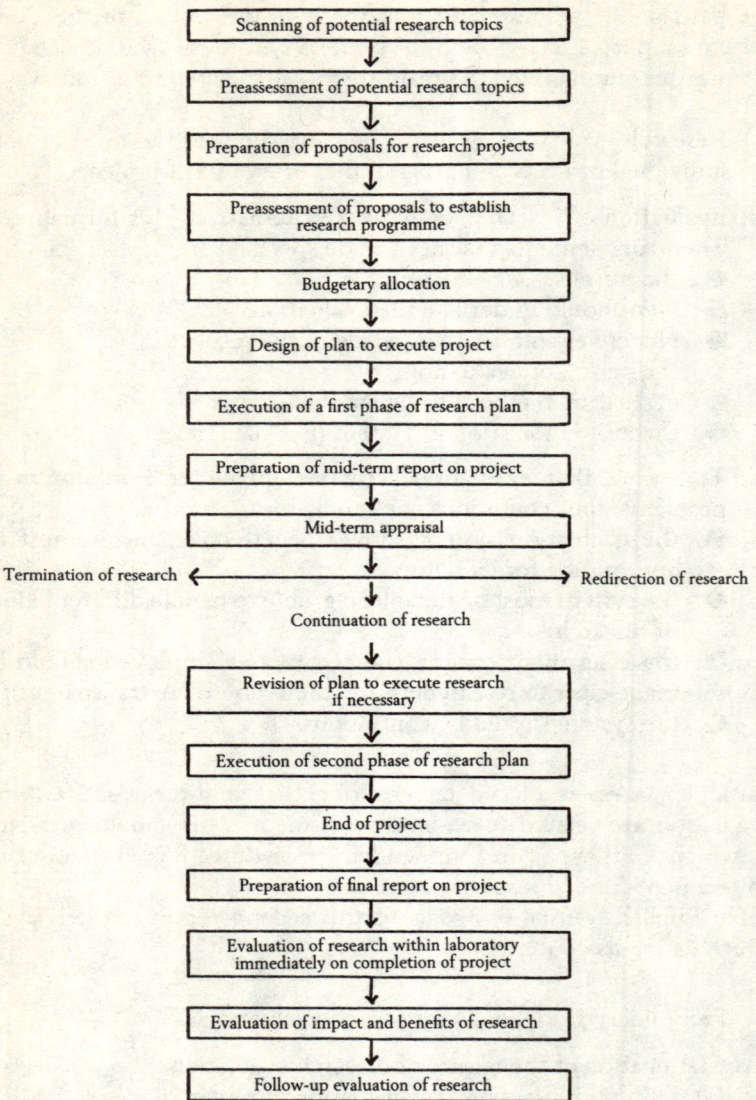

Figure 3 Recommended evaluation procedure in national laboratories
Source: Council for Science and Technology (1986b, p. 33)

  (d) The need to define the scope of research evaluation
3 Points to note in the construction of a research evaluation system
  (a) The desirable features of a research evaluation system
  (b) Points to note in actually setting up a research evaluation system
4 Determining the structural elements of a research evaluation system
  (a) Method of determining structural elements
  (b) The need to improve previous practice in research evaluation

Appendix — Actual examples of research evaluation systems

 The official interviewed reported that one of the major problems in developing guidelines for evaluation arose from the fact that different criteria need to be employed for different types of research. In the case of more basic research, the emphasis should be placed on assessing its innovative aspects, while in very applied or development work the principal criterion for success is efficiency in meeting pre-established technical goals. Consequently, an important first step was to develop an acceptable research classification scheme. The following definitions were used:

> 'basic' — research carried out in order to gain fundamentally new scientific knowledge by analyzing principles and phenomena;
>
> 'non-basic' — research utilizing scientific knowledge which has already been explained;
>
> 'applied' — research carried out for a specific purpose;
>
> 'non-applied' — research undertaken for a non-targeted purpose.

Four 'types' of research were then identified using the 2 × 2 matrix outlined in Figure 4: 'basic non-applied research' (type 1); 'basic applied research' (type 2, often termed in the CST reports as 'basic research included in development'); 'non-basic applied research' (type 3); and 'non-basic, non-applied research' (type 4).[13] The official stressed that evaluation of type 2 research is seen as especially problematic since it is normally undertaken as part of a wider development programme. The extent to which the basic science is in place in the different components of the programme (often taking the form of 'projects') varies, and in some the research needs to be tackled at a very fundamental level — that is, the research is 'contingent'. Since the

	Basic	Non-Basic
Applied	*Type 2* – 'basic applied research' or 'basic research included in development'. Contingent or strategic research where new scientific knowledge is produced to fulfil specified goals or technical targets. Relatively high scientific uncertainty involved.	*Type 3* – 'non-basic applied research'. Aims to reach well specified technical targets utilizing already acquired scientific knowledge. Lower degree of scientific uncertainty involved but technical uncertainty can be high.
Non-Applied	*Type 1* – 'basic non-applied research'. Undertaken for acquisition of new knowledge or basic principles without regard to subsequent use. Primarily fundamental research but can include strategic elements. Very high scientific uncertainty involved.	*Type 4* – 'non-basic, non-applied research'. Residual category covering secondary data analysis, measurement and observation techniques, etc. Low degree of scientific and technical uncertainty involved.

Figure 4 Research classification scheme employed by Council for Science and Technology
Source: CST (1986b, Chapter 1, and Figure 1, p. 4). See also Stokes (1982, p. 17).

overall programme evaluation must ultimately focus on application, this often results in the contributions made by the more basic project elements being ignored. Special attention was thus given to developing criteria for evaluating the 'seeds of innovative and supreme work'.

The next step in developing guidelines was to produce sets of criteria relevant to assessing the four types of research. These were then incorporated into sample checklists and forms that could easily be adopted by institutes without evaluation systems. These have been created with the assessment of medium-sized programmes in mind, that is, those costing between $3 million and $30 million over a five-year period.

The approach here was to develop two sets of 'profile formats', one for preassessment and the other for mid-term or post-hoc assessment.

Each consists of five separate forms: (a) 'overall format describing research'; (b) 'analytical format for basic research'; (c) 'analytical format for development' (i.e. 'non-basic research'); (d) 'analytical format for basic research included in development' (i.e. 'basic applied research'); and (e) 'total evaluation format'. For each type of research, several forms are employed—thus, for preassessment of type 2 research, the relevant forms (a), (c), (d) and (e) are required, while (a), (c) and (e) are used for type 3 (see CST 1986b, Tables 2 and 3, p. 29).

The criteria specified in the preassessment forms appear to be wide-ranging and comprehensive. To take an example of form (d) for 'basic research included in development', evaluators are asked to make comments on and rank the following using a four-point scale:

(a) Content of research
- Innovativeness
- Quality of content and methods
- Extent to which research and methods contribute to development of field
- Likely direct scientific or technological impacts
- Likely indirect scientific or technological impacts
- Extent to which research contributes to mission of laboratory

(b) R&D plan
- Extent to which goal is clearly identified
- Extent to which goals are adequate and appropriate
- Extent to which research plan is satisfactory (timing, methods, procedures, techniques)

(c) Other criteria (to be specified)

As noted above, this form needs to be used in conjunction with others, in particular with a schedule (c) for 'development' activities. Although including some of the same criteria (e.g. 'innovativeness' and 'mission relevance'), its orientation is rather more practically focused. The criteria employed include:

- How necessary is the research—is it high or low in terms of economic or social priorities, technology or resource requirements, or other needs (to be specified)?
- Is the proposed research in accord with overall governmental R&D priorities?
- How urgent is the research?
- Is the research plan adequate in relation to the proposed

budget, facilities and equipment required, available researchers, and schedule of work?
- Are the 'basic seeds' for the research appropriate and sufficient?
- Has adequate prior screening and scanning of research underway in other laboratories been carried out?
- Are there any constraints on the research (e.g. social acceptability)?
- Will it be difficult to achieve the proposed target from the viewpoint of the research involved?
- What is the expectation of success (as a percentage of risk that the research will not be completed satisfactorily)?
- Has an acceptable mid-term evaluation target been set?

The criteria suggested for mid-term and ex-post evaluation are, however, somewhat less comprehensive. For example, the general assessment form (a) requests information on:

- title of project or programme;
- name of principal researcher;
- time period of research;
- phase of evaluation in the research plan;
- research budget, numbers of researchers, and capital investment undertaken;
- category of research (types 1–4);
- nature of research support ('ordinary research', 'special research', 'commissioned research', other);
- results from project anticipated in original proposal;
- unplanned, unexpected or secondary results;
- details of publications;
- any other information of note.

The related form (c) for 'development' requests rankings on a four-point scale of the following criteria:

- Has the research proceeded in line with the schedule set out in the plan?
- Have the expected results been achieved?
- Have important unexpected or secondary results been achieved?
- Have there been any scientific or technical developments likely to affect the target for the research?

- Have there been any socio-economic changes likely to affect the target for the research?
- Is the target specified in the research plan still appropriate?
- Are the proposed research methods and techniques still appropriate?
- Are there any other problems likely to influence achievement of the research targets?
- Any other points of note.

It is too early to assess the extent to which the various sets of guidelines and forms will actually be used in evaluation, although it should be noted that implementation has already taken place in the programme on Special Co-ordination Funds for Science and Technology administered by the Science and Technology Agency (see Chapter 4 below).

While the officials and staff interviewed were generally positive about the initiative, reservations were expressed in the larger AIST research centres that the guidelines, especially those for mid-term or ex-post evaluation, are too simplistic and mechanistic. The response of the STA official was that they expected AIST institutes to be more critical since a higher proportion of their funding comes in the form of block grants while the guidelines are primarily concerned with evaluating individual projects or programmes. It was also stressed that the aim of the guidelines initiative was to promote evaluation *within* institutes and horizontally across collaborative programmes, and clearly some organizations need more assistance with developing assessment procedures than others. Moreover, the guidelines are advisory and are intended to complement, not supplant, vertical evaluation by ministries (for example, the MITI 'Industrial Technology Council' is responsible for assessing AIST institutes) or by the Administrative Inspection Bureau.

As to the possible problems arising from reliance by laboratories on what is basically internal review, the STA view is that most assessment tasks can be undertaken satisfactorily in-house provided that this is complemented by regular external review as well as evaluation by funding agencies of the programmes they support. The CST guidelines do, however, suggest that, where research is 'new or very basic', laboratories should be encouraged to involve third parties (external committee members or reviewers) in the assessment.

Finally, both the STA official and others interviewed in the study stressed that one of the main points of the CST exercise was to promote national debate on how to improve research evaluation. In this respect, it certainly seems to have succeeded.[14]

Notes

1. The CST has significant influence within the Japanese government. As Lynn (1986, p. 298) observes, 'in some respects the CST is an inner cabinet. Its Chairman is the Prime Minister, and its members include the Ministers from Finance and Education, and the Director-Generals of the Science and Technology Agency and the Economic Planning Agency. The other members are the Chairman of the Science Council of Japan and five members of "outstanding ability" from the scientific community. These members of the "scientific community", it should be noted, also provide a linkage to big business.' In 1987, two were the presidents of major corporations (Kansai Electric Power and Mitsubishi Shipbuilding and Engineering) and one a recently retired company president (ex NTT).
2. Between 1969 and 1979, for example, spending on national laboratories quadrupled while funding per researcher rose by 350 per cent (Kodama et al., 1981, p. 2).
3. This point is also stressed by Tanaka (1987) in explaining the recent interest in Japan with R&D evaluation. Also regarded as important is the increasing emphasis of government on the support of more basic technological research and the consequent demands this places on existing evaluation systems.
4. One interviewee stated that, despite the official extension of AIB's powers in recent years, its scope for making radical recommendations is still in practice somewhat limited. Such decisions would need to be acceptable to the relevant committees in the agency concerned. Far more power can be exercised by the Ministry of Finance during the annual round of budgetary discussions with agencies.
5. There is no specific requirement for staff to have a background in science and technology. The inspector currently in charge of the division has a first degree in law and the assistant inspector a degree in management science.
6. AIB staff expressed the view that effective evaluation of institutes can be undertaken without examining the content of individual research projects provided that 'hearings' take place with relevant experts and the industrial or governmental 'user-community'.
7. The AIB 'Medium-Term Inspection Plan on Research Activities' shows that inspections of eight government laboratories and public research corporations were scheduled to begin before the end of 1987, while a further eight are planned for 1988 and six for 1989. Reports have still to be produced on the eleven inspections commenced in 1986.
8. RIKEN has been given responsibility for running the new 'Frontier

Research Programme' on life sciences (Institute of Physical and Chemical Research 1986).
9. This point is reinforced by Tanaka (1987, p. 20) who states that 'unless higher authorities request the evaluation, its nature often tends to in-house type evaluations in the sense that the same authorities initiate projects and bear responsibility for them . . . The researchers have little incentive to expose themselves to evaluation as the Japanese seniority system often prevents them from receiving special promotion or an increase in research expenditure as a result of positive evaluation of their research. They may perceive that there is more demerit when they are unsuccessful in their research than merit in the case of success.'
10. The Council for Science and Technology is comprised of a General Meeting chaired by the Prime Minister together with a Steering Committee and Committee on Policy Matters. Most activities are undertaken within seven panels (for example, on General Planning and Research Objectives). Reporting to the Committee on Policy Matters are three Sub-Committees on Basic Survey, Research Survey and Research Evaluation (see Yoshimura, 1987).
11. The other members are S Watanabe (Tokyo Cosmopolitan Science and Technology University), T Akashi (Aginomoto Corporation), A Arami (Tokyo University), A Ichikawa (Tokyo Institute of Technology), M Uenohara (Nihon Denki Corporation), K Matsui (Rikkyo University) and S Yoshida (RIKEN). The Committee is serviced by staff from the Science and Technology Agency. In addition, a working party chaired by Professor F Kodama (Saitama University) was set up by STA to provide background material on research evaluation to the Committee. This also has a wide-ranging membership: T Ikegama (NTT), Y Inomata (National Institute for Research in Inorganic Materials), H Osada (Asahi Research Centre), N Araya (National Research Institute for Metals), M Suzuki (Shin Nihon Steel Corporation), T Miyakawa (RIKEN) and F Yoshinaga (Ajinomoto Corporation).
12. It may well be worth DTI considering translating both this report and the second on 'Guidelines for Research Evaluation'. Although the costs of translation from Japanese to English are high, the combined length of the documents, including appendices and tables, is only 140 pages.
13. In general terms, type 2 research can be regarded as equivalent to the category of 'strategic applied research' employed by the Department of Trade and Industry, while type 3 equates broadly with 'specific applied research' — see note 4 in Chapter 1.
14. One indicator of the growing interest in research evaluation was the establishment in 1986 of a 'Society for Science Policy and Research Management'. This has a membership of around 300 drawn mainly from government and industry, and publishes its own *Journal of Science Policy and Research Management*.

3
Evaluation of Applied Research in MITI Agency of Industrial Science and Technology (AIST)

Structure and Organization of AIST

The central mission of AIST is to promote the development of industrial science and technology in Japan. Besides operating a network of sixteen laboratories, it funds a variety of national R&D programmes spanning the government and private sectors, assists technological development in companies through a system of conditional loans, tax concessions and grants, and stimulates the diffusion into industry of new technology developed within its research programmes.[1] The organizational structure of the Agency is shown in Figure 5, while a breakdown of its 1986 budget of $820 million is given in Figure 6.

Given the wide range of AIST's support for strategic and applied research, it was necessary to focus on selected programmes and institutes. As noted in Chapter 1, those chosen for detailed study were The Basic Technology for Future Industries Programme, The Large-Scale R&D Programme, and four AIST institutes — the National Research Laboratory of Metrology, the Mechanical Engineering Laboratory, the Electrotechnical Laboratory, and the National Chemical Laboratory for Industry. Let us consider how research evaluation is carried out within each of them in turn.

Basic Technology for Future Industries Programme

Outline of Programme

Initiated in 1981, the programme aims to develop 'revolutionary basic technology essential to the establishment of new industries which are expected to flourish in the 1990s' (AIST 1987, p. 1). Eleven projects

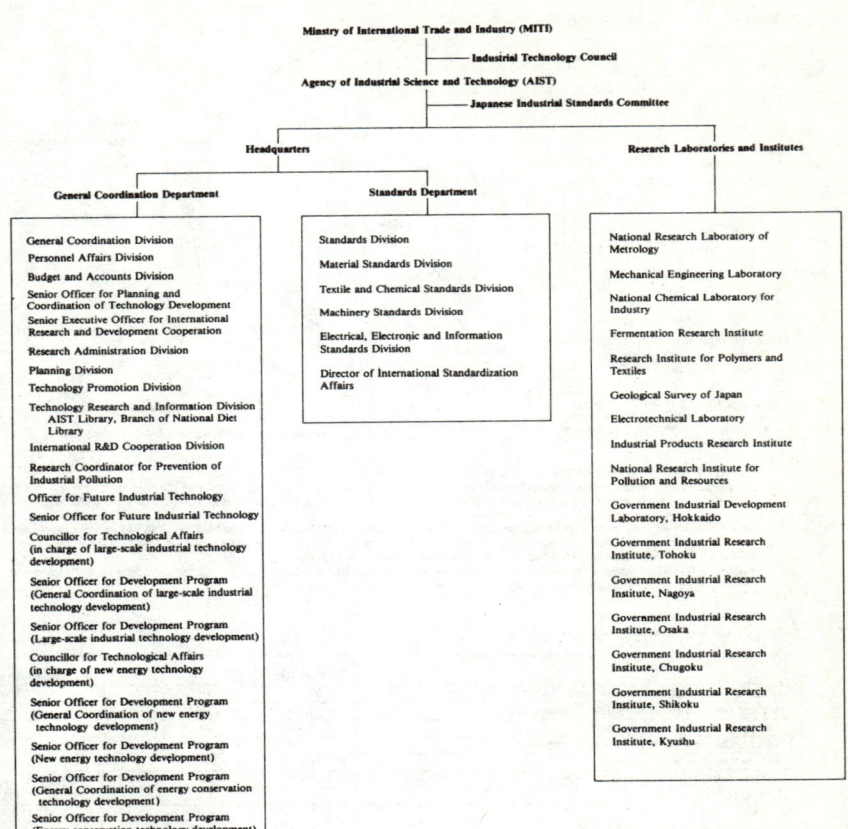

Figure 5 Organization of Agency of Industrial Science and Technology
Source: AIST (1986a, p. 1)

36 Evaluation of Applied Research in AIST

1. Budget

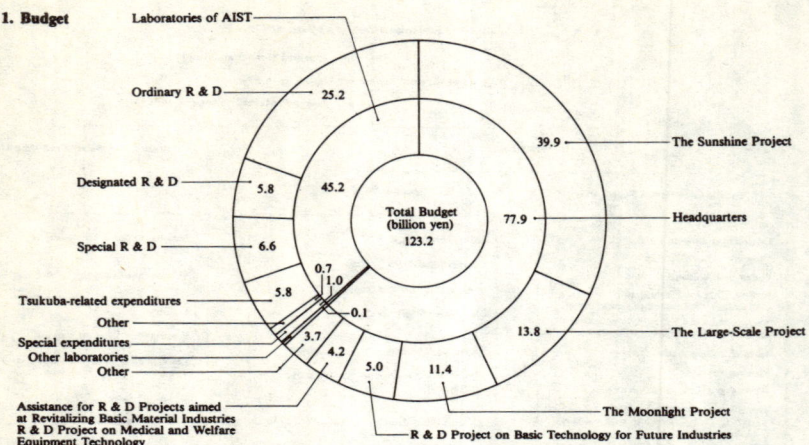

Note: **Ordinary R & D:** Personnel exenditures and ordinary research expenditures of AIST laboratories.
Designated R & D: Research expenditures incurred by research laboratories through work connected with the Large-Scale Project, the Sunshine and Moonlight Projects, R & D Project on Medical and Welfare Equipment Technology, R & D Project on Basic Technologies for Future Industries and the Regional Large-Scale Project.
Special R & D: Expenditures incurred through Special research, Expansion of Laboratory Facilities, Operation of Geological Research Vessel, Nuclear Research, R & D Promotion for Small Industries, Research Related to Prevention of Environmental Pollution.
Tsukuba related expenditures: Expenditures in operating joint facilities at Tsukuba.
Budget for individual projects: This refers to the total budget for each of the Large Scale Project, Sunshine and Moonlight Projects and R & D Project on Basic Technology for Future Industries.

2. Budget and Personnel for each Laboratories

	Budget (million yen)	Personnel	Researchers	Administrators
Agency of Industrial Science and Technology (Headquarters)	77,930	320	0	320
National Research Laboratory of Metrology	2,151	226	128	98
Mechanical Engineering Laboratory	3,313	290	221	69
National Chemical Laboratory for Industry	3,794	370	287	83
Fermentation Research Institute	1,629	88	69	19
Research Institute for Polymers and Textiles	1,445	127	104	23
Geological Survey of Japan	4,464	379	248	131
Electrotechnical Laboratory	8,763	697	558	139
Industrial Products Research Institute	1,521	131	104	27
National Research Institute for Pollution and Resources	3,850	341	248	93
Government Industrial Development Laboratory, Hokkaido	1,184	99	74	25
Government Industrial Research Institute, Tohoku	630	56	39	17
Government Industrial Research Institute, Nagoya	2,496	255	196	59
Government Industrial Research Institute, Osaka	2,711	228	175	53
Government Industrial Research Institute, Chugoku	732	52	40	12
Government Industrial Research Institute, Shikoku	466	45	34	11
Government Industrial Research Institute, Kyushu	855	90	69	21
Common Expenditures	5,164	–	–	–
Other Laboratories	130	–	–	–
Total	123,228	3,794	2,594	1,200

Figure 6 Budget and personnel of Agency of Industrial Science and Technology, fiscal year 1986
Source: AIST (1986a, p. 4)

Table 2 Organizational participation in Basic Technology for Future Industries Programme

Project Title	Private Sector Participants	Public Sector Participants
High Performance Ceramics	Engineering Research Association for High Performance Ceramics	Government Industrial Research Institute, Nagoya Government Industrial Research Institute, Osaka Mechanical Engineering Laboratory National Institute for Research in Inorganic Materials
Synthetic Membranes for New Separation Technology	Research Association of Polymer Basic Technology	National Chemical Laboratory of Industry Industrial Products Research Institute Research Institute for Polymers and Textiles
Synthetic Metals	Research Association of Polymer Basic Technology	Electrotechnical Laboratory Research Institute for Polymers and Textiles
High Performance Plastics	Research Association of Polymer Basic Technology	Research Institute for Polymers and Textiles
Advanced Alloys with Controlled Crystalline Structures	Research and Development Institute for Metals and Composites for Future Industries	Mechanical Engineering Laboratory Government Industrial Research Institute, Nagoya National Research Institute for Metals
Advanced Composite Materials	Research and Development Institute for Metals and Composites for Future Industries	Industrial Products Research Institute Mechanical Engineering Laboratory Research Institute for Polymers and Textiles Government Industrial Research Institute, Osaka
Bioreactors	Research Association for Biotechnology	Fermentation Research Institute Research Institute for Polymers and Textiles National Chemical Laboratory of Industry
Large Scale Cell Cultivation	Research Association for Biotechnology	
Utilizing Recombinant DNA	Research Association for Biotechnology	Fermentation Research Institute Research Institute for Polymers and Textiles National Chemical Laboratory of Industry
Superlattice Devices	Research and Development Association for Future Electronic Devices	Electrotechnical Laboratory
Three Dimensional ICs	Research and Development Association for Future Electronic Devices	Electrotechnical Laboratory
Fortified ICs for Extreme Conditions	Research and Development Association for Future Electronic Devices	Electrotechnical Laboratory

Source: AIST (1987, p. 11)

are currently being supported covering the fields of new materials, biotechnology and new electronic devices. Each is in an area which has 'theoretically or experimentally shown potential for application in new industrial technologies' (ibid.) but which would be too risky or costly for an individual firm to undertake alone. R&D is conducted from the basic stage right up to the point where projects are beginning to yield technologies or materials ready for practical application.

Before considering the procedures used to assess research, one should be aware of some of the main features of the programme since the planning, management and evaluation functions are strongly interrelated. First, all projects involve collaborative R&D between AIST institutes and groups of industrial companies. Firms are in most cases organized within a 'research association' which has line responsibility for managing the project. The structure of organizational participation within the various projects is shown in Table 2.

Second, significant effort is devoted over a long period to choosing projects which are normally conceived within research associations and proposed to AIST by a consortium of interested companies and institutes. Whilst the Agency in principle meets the full costs of industrial participation, the funds given are generally insufficient. The fact that companies are both intimately involved in project definition and have to finance some of their participation costs ensures the 'industrial relevance' of the research. Projects selected for support have to fit into the research themes identified by the AIST Industrial Technology Council as technologically important for the future.

Third, all projects have a planned duration of ten years which is divided into three distinct phases: basic conceptual and theoretical research; development of candidate prototype technologies, devices or sample materials; and further development of the most promising options. Although participants are fully involved throughout the project, the typical pattern of activity is that institutes are more active in the first two phases, while companies invest greater time and resources in the second and third.

Finally, each project has a long-term plan drawn up by a specially appointed 'Development Committee' in collaboration with participants. This consists of representatives from the academic community, government institutes and research associations, and determines the themes of research and a schedule of work. The plan normally sets out relatively detailed technical aims, for example specifying the minimum levels of operation under particular physical conditions (space, temperature, pressure, and so on).

According to the AIST official interviewed, the existence of detailed technical aims makes the task of evaluation simpler because the outcomes can be readily related to intentions. Much effort is put into assessment — which is undertaken by an 'Evaluation Committee' (EC) set up for each project — because of pressures to use resources effectively and demonstrate that high quality research has been produced.

EC membership is drawn primarily from recognized technical experts in national universities, government institutes and research associations. There is a strict rule that no direct industrial participation is allowed since members have to be independent and free from constraints of commercial confidentiality. Membership is on the basis of extendable one-year terms. Unlike in most other programmes, the EC reports to the Director of AIST rather than to the Industrial Technology Council.

Procedures for Evaluation

Three main types of evaluation are undertaken. The most routine is the annual assessment of progress when decisions are formally made on the continuation of funding for individual elements of projects. This includes examination by the EC of the performance of individual researchers from both institutes and companies. Although administratively important, annual evaluations are rarely used to make major decisions affecting the future of projects.

Most important are the mid-term assessments which take place after the first and second phases of each project. At both stages, rigorous evaluation is carried out by the Evaluation Committee (in close consultation with the research association involved) to decide which candidate technologies, techniques or materials should be selected for further study and which should be discontinued. The extent to which technical aims have been, or are likely to be, achieved is the main assessment criterion. Interestingly, a decision was taken in 1986 to terminate the project on Fortified ICs for Extreme Conditions just over half-way through its planned duration — not because of failure but because the project had *already* surpassed its technical goals. Conversely, we were told, if a project was not proceeding satisfactorily, 'for example, because the methodology and techniques proposed could not possibly reach the target, we would end it immediately'. An example of the approach used to compare progress

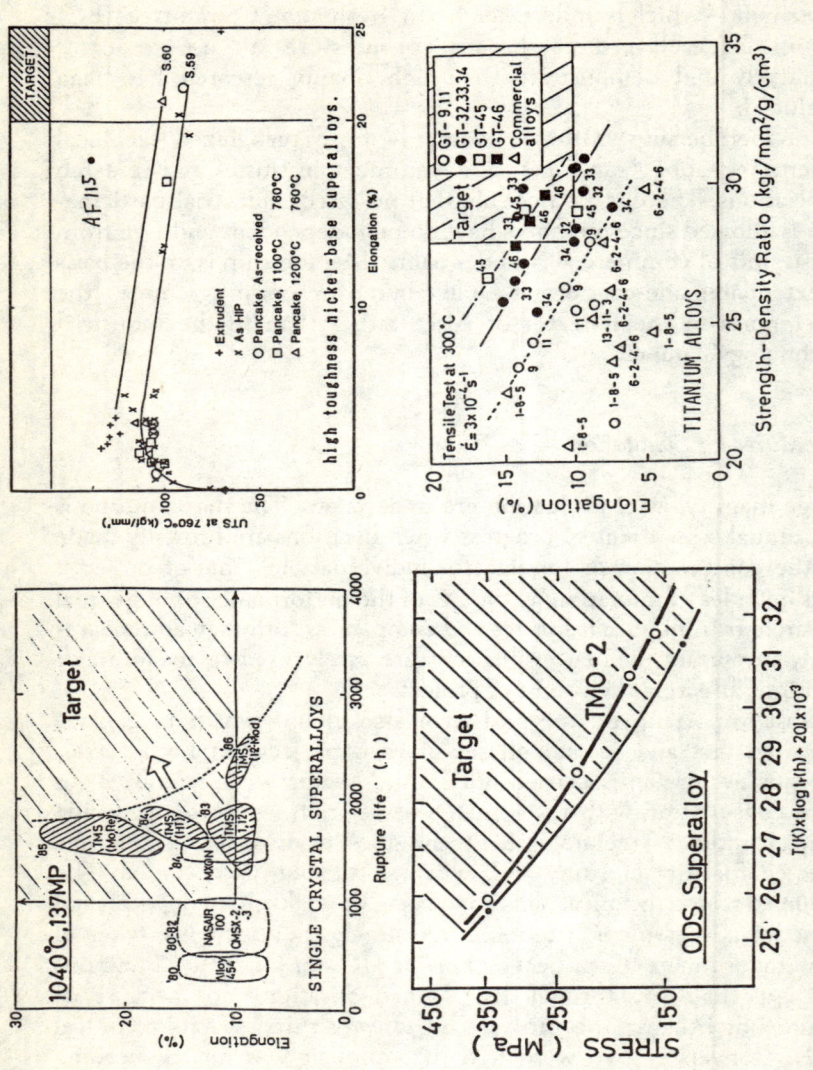

Figure 7 Technical targets of Jisedai Project and results obtained in designed alloys
Source: National Research Institute for Metals (n.d.). See also Research and Development Institute of Metals and Composites for Future Industries (1984).

achieved with the initial technical aims is given in Figure 7 which relates to the Jisedai Project on Advanced Alloys with Controlled Crystalline Structures (National Research Institute for Metals, n.d.)

The third type of assessment takes place in the final year of projects. Three sessions of the EC are held after which a draft evaluation report is produced in consultation with the Development Committee. This is then sent to half a dozen academic experts for comment on the technical merits of the work. After revision, the evaluation report is submitted to the Director-General of AIST.

Concerning the use of quantitative indicators of research output, the AIST official interviewed stated that records are kept of patent applications as well as numbers of published papers and conference presentations. However, none of these are regarded as especially important. Rather, he stressed that 'the decisive factor is whether or not a particular technical level is reached'. As for quantitatively assessing the success of projects in terms of financial benefits to companies, the official felt this to be wholly unsuitable. In longer-term applied research, it takes time for tangible benefits to appear and their diffuse nature presents severe measurement problems. Furthermore, the experts on the Evaluation Committee are regarded as well able to judge if the completed research has been executed successfully and whether the results are likely to find industrial application.

Case Study of Evaluation

It is useful to complement the picture of evaluation given by the AIST official with the views of an industrial participant. Dr S Kataoka, Corporate Director and Divisional General Manager of Sharp Central Research Laboratories, was instrumental in initiating the 'Project on Three-Dimensional ICs' while running the Electronic Device Division of the Electrotechnical Laboratory (ETL). This project aims to develop a fundamentally new integrated-circuit technology in which elements are integrated in three rather than in two dimensions. By achieving parallel processing between two-dimensional layers, the intention is to create intelligent sensors capable of performing complex information-intensive functions such as acting as an artificial retina — see, for example, Kataoka (1986a, 1986b).

Setting up the project took nearly ten years of 'often heated' monthly discussions within a group of academics, AIST officials, institute researchers and industrialists who met informally under the aegis of the Japan Association for the Promotion of the Electronic Industry. This is much longer than the normal project definition period of two to three years before consensus is reached on technical aims and participants and a proposal submitted to AIST for funding. Underlying the discussions, according to Kataoka, was a recognition of the longer-term limitations of traditional integrated-circuit technology and the 'desire no longer to follow the basic electronic technologies of the US — we wanted a new Japanese technological paradigm'.

The project involves collaboration between ETL and a consortium of seven major Japanese electronics companies organized within the Research and Development Association for Future Electronic Devices. Day-to-day management is vested in a 'project coordinator' based at ETL (Kataoka performed this function before moving to Sharp).

As usual, the project was divided into three phases. The first was a four-year feasibility study to establish the basic techniques required, the most important of which was silicon-on-insulator (SOI) technology. Partly as a result of their differing commercial requirements, the various participants preferred separate approaches to developing this technology so it was decided to experiment with seven methods in parallel (see Table 3). This was done competitively, with significant prestige for the company producing the most successful solution, but on the understanding that all participants would share the resultant technology. In this way, penalties for individual companies attempting risky but innovative research were kept to a minimum, while maximising the potential benefits to the consortium as a whole. Kataoka identified this as a central element in the organization of the project.

At the end of the first phase, assessment showed that two of the candidate approaches (those of Firms D and F) were particularly promising and these were selected for further development. As work progressed within the second phase, the choice was narrowed to the 'poly-si-cap' technique pioneered by Firm F. This is now yielding satisfactory results and has, Kataoka believes, 'established the foundations for a fundamental new technology'.

Concerning the evaluation approach employed, Kataoka argued that the crucial element was the use of two mid-term assessments. It was also important that they were carried out by an independent 'Evaluation Committee' comprised of experts with no commercial interest in the research. He stressed the part played by the 'project coordinator' in preparing for such assessments, as well as in more routine monitoring and evaluation to identify emerging problems.

Table 3 Goals and candidate technical approaches in 3-D Project

Organization	SOI Technology	Target Device
Firm A	E-beam	High speed logic
Firm B	Laser split-beam	High density memory
Firm C	GaAs on Si	Something new
Firm D	Selective antireflection laser	Intelligent image sensor
Firm E	Dual laser-beam, heat sink	Intelligent image sensor
Firm F	Poly-Si cap, laser M-shaped laser-beam	Intelligent image sensor
Firm G	Spinel on Si	Intelligent image sensor
ETL	Basic technology — SOR lithography — Ion-beam process — New device, etc.	Intelligent image sensor

Source: Unpublished material produced by the Research and Development Association for Future Electronic Devices

Although administratively necessary, the annual assessment required by AIST was regarded as of lesser importance.

Kataoka also expressed agreement with the AIST policy of concentrating on technical outcomes in evaluation, although the fundamental nature of the research meant that detailed targets could not be set at the outset of the project. Counts of papers in international journals, conference presentations and patents were all seen as useful indicators of technical progress, and are indeed used in his own company's laboratory. However, success ultimately needs to be judged by technical experts, and in this respect the evaluation approach employed by AIST was considered satisfactory. Kataoka in particular did not wish to see financial 'rate-of-return' calculations used to assess the impact of research on industry, feeling that this was inappropriate for longer-term government-funded research. He also saw a danger in 'over-evaluation' which can lead to 'loss of freedom' and a tendency towards conservatism among researchers.

Large-Scale R&D Programme[2]

Outline of Programme

The Large-Scale Programme was established in 1966 to support work on 'technical themes which are of particular importance and urgency to the nation as a whole' (AIST 1986a, p. 6). In its first fifteen years, the emphasis was on long-term development projects such as the high-performance electronic computer (1966–71) and remotely controlled undersea oil-drilling rig (1970–5). Since 1981, the trend has been to support more basic and strategic (but still industrially related) research — for example, on advanced robot technology. Details of current and completed projects are given in Tables 4 and 5.

The AIST Industrial Technology Council is responsible for overall management of the Large-Scale Programme, including policy formulation and selection of new projects. Within the Council, there is a 'Large-Scale Programme Committee' with nine subcommittees responsible for each current project. There is also an Evaluation Subcomittee whose activities are discussed below.

From the outset, the emphasis has been on interdisciplinary R&D, and on projects acting as bridges between government institutes, universities and industry. Five criteria are used for selecting projects which must be concerned with R&D that

- is urgently required for upgrading national industrial standards, promoting efficient utilization of natural resources, preventing industrial pollution, etc.;
- is expected to make a significant impact on the development of manufacturing and mining industries;
- cannot be undertaken by private firms because of the major investment requirements, long-term commitment to funding, high risk, absence of profit motive, etc.;
- has clearly specified targets and well-examined attainment prospects;
- can be carried out by government institutes in collaboration with industry and universities (AIST 1986a, p. 3).

The usual form of project organization is a consortium of industrial companies working together with one or more government institutes. All are given contracts for specified R&D tasks, with the institutes and any university participants being responsible for the more basic research.

Table 4 AIST Large-Scale R&D Programme — ongoing projects

Project	R&D period (FY)	Total R&D expenditure (millions of yen)	Budget for FY 1985
C_1 chemical technology	1980–86	10,500	1,022
Manganese nodule mining system	1981–89	20,000	958
High-speed computer system for scientific and technological uses	1981–89	23,000	2,889
Automated sewing system	1981–90	10,000	1,341
Advanced robot technology	1983–90	20,000	2,405
Observation system for Earth Resources Satellite-1	1984–90	23,000	4,391
New water treatment system	1985–90	11,800	1,072
Interoperable database system	1985–91	15,000	831
Advanced material processing and machining system	1986–	—	20

Source: AIST (1986b, p. 15)

Approach to Evaluation

Considerable efforts have been made in recent years to institute more systematic evaluation within the Large-Scale Programme. However, the AIST official responsible for the programme stressed how difficult this had proved given the wide diversity in projects supported — they range from relatively basic research to experimental development and relate to industrial sectors as different as ocean mining technology and chemical plant engineering.

The stimulus to improve assessment has come not just from the concern with accountability in R&D spending, but from experience with certain longer-running projects. In particular, AIST found that the project on C1 Chemical Technology, which aims to replace petrochemical products with coal and natural gas derivatives, was yielding technically successful results that were nevertheless unlikely

Table 5 AIST Large-Scale R&D Programme – completed projects

Project	R&D period (FY)	Total R&D expenditure (millions of yen)	Outline of project
Super-high-performance electronic computer	1966–71	10,100	Large-scale computer system with super-high performance
Desulphurization process	1966–71	2,700	(1) Efficient removal of the SO_2 contained in the waste gases from power or other plants (2) Direct removal of sulphur from heavy oil
New method of producing olefins	1967–72	1,200	Economic production of olefins by direct cracking of crude oil instead of using naphtha
Remotely controlled undersea oil drilling ring	1970–75	4,500	Remote-control oil-drilling rigs for under-sea use
Sea-water desalination and by-product recovery	1969–77	7,000	Economical large-scale production of fresh water and economical by-product recovery technology
Electric car	1971–77	5,700	Various types of electric car to replace ordinary vehicles in urban areas
Comprehensive automobile control technology	1973–79	7,400	Integrated control technology with a view to relieving traffic congestion, reducing automobile pollution and traffic accidents, etc.
Pattern information processing system	1971–80	22,100	Computer technology for the recognition and processing of pattern information such as characters, pictures, objects and speech
Direct steelmaking process using high-temperature reducing gas	1973–80	14,000	Direct steelmaking technology aimed at a closed-system which uses the heat energy from a multi-purpose high temperature gas-cooled reactor in the steelmaking process

Evaluation of Applied Research in AIST 47

Table 5 – *cont.*

Project	R&D period (FY)	Total R&D expenditure (millions of yen)	Outline of project
Olefin production from heavy oil as raw material	1975–81	14,200	Technology for manufacturing high-value-added olefins (commonly known as ethylene, propylene, etc.) using a high sulphur-content heavy oil fraction (so-called asphalt), which is difficult to desulphurize, as the raw material
Jet engines for aircraft	1971–75 (1st phase) 1976–81 (2nd phase)	6,900 12,900	Research and development of large-scale turbofan engine designed for use in commercial transports in the 1980s
Resource recovery technology	1973–75 (1st phase) 1976–82 (2nd phase)	1,300 11,400	R&D on technical systems for the disposal of solid urban waste, centred on resource recycling with a view to promoting the efficient utilization of resources and facilitating the smooth application of solid urban waste treatment
Flexible manufacturing system complex provided with laser	1977–84	13,500	R&D on new, automatic, integrated production systems that are flexible and provide quick throughput in the manufacture of small batches of machine components
Subsea oil production system	1978–84	17,200	R&D on an efficient system for subsea oil production which would be applicable to the continental shelf and slope surrounding Japan and to deep-sea oil fields
Optical measurement and control system	1979–85	15,700	R&D on an optical measurement and control system permitting massive volumes of data, including picture images, to be measured and controlled in adverse environments

Source: AIST (1986b, p. 15)

to be taken up by industry in the near future. The project, which was planned in the late 1970s and ran during 1980–6 at a cost of $70 million, did not have any built-in procedure for mid-term evaluation. Consequently, it proved difficult to steer the work in new directions to take in account the impact of lower world energy prices and the effects of yen revaluation.

As with other AIST programmes, a great deal of emphasis is placed on the project-planning stage (generally termed 'preassessment'). This is the responsibility of the relevant subcommittee within the Industrial Technology Council. Using the results of technological surveys of the field in question, the subcommittee develops detailed technical goals in consultation with the interested research communities in government institutes and industry. In the past, apart from routine monitoring[3] and review of progress undertaken prior to the annual budget discussions, assessment took place only at the end of projects when the final report was submitted, and was principally concerned with checking whether the technical goals had been achieved.

The assessment procedure employed has, however, been strengthened since 1982. As noted above, there is now a formally constituted 'Evaluation Subcommittee' responsible for both mid-term and final assessment of all projects. This has ten members drawn from universities, research institutes and industry, who are appointed on two-year renewable terms. Mid-term evaluation is carried out three years into projects which normally have a fixed lifetime of six years. Final evaluation is undertaken during the last year.

Given their diversity, no attempt has been made to develop detailed assessment criteria applicable to all projects.[4] The approach is still to assess results primarily in terms of whether they meet the technical goals originally specified. However, greater stress is now being placed on evaluating the take-up of technology by industry, especially by companies participating in projects. The AIST official interviewed felt that the Evaluation Subcommittee was able to undertake this task adequately given its close links with industry and the informal integration of participating companies within the decision-making process. As recent projects have a more basic orientation, it is recognized that it will also be necessary to evaluate the 'fundamentality' of the results produced and their 'potential for future application'. These are regarded as more difficult to measure. Previously, the process of implementation had normally begun before projects ended.

As for the use of quantitative indicators in judging the impact of projects, the official reported that the number and quality of patents was an important input to evaluation. Records of subsequent royalty income are also kept.[5] Although counts of papers and reports are formally made, these play little role in determining the extent to which a project is regarded as having been a success. Nor is any attempt made by AIST to quantify the financial impact on companies of the technology developed within the programme. This is because at the time of assessment the impact is usually still too far upstream in a company's activities, and therefore too difficult to measure.

Case Study of Evaluation

One recently completed project within the Large-Scale Programme was on optical measurement and control systems. Carried out by the Electrotechnical Laboratory in association with ten companies (including Hitachi and Sumitomo), the aim was to develop a Japanese capability in opto-electronic materials and devices equal to the world state-of-the-art. The project focused in particular on optical techniques for measuring, monitoring and controlling large volumes of data, including visual information, generated in industrial plants and other sites with adverse environments (for example, where radiation or inflammable gases are present). There was a significant basic component to the research, especially in relation to integrated optics and laser wave-guides. The project ran from 1979 to 1985 and cost just over $100 million.

Assessment of the project was completed by the Evaluation Sub-committee in August 1986 (Industrial Technology Council, 1986). However, the evaluation report is not publicly available and it was only possible to obtain brief details during the visit to AIST. The overall conclusion, according to the AIST official interviewed, is that the project was most successful and indeed was terminated a year earlier than planned.[6] The assessment report shows that all the original targets specified were met in full. These were that the system should transmit data using optical fibres from a distance greater than 100 metres and with an image point matrix of 1000 x 1000; be capable of operating with at least twenty terminals in each trans-mission network; and have a minimum transmission speed of one gigabit per second. Although these targets were set in 1979 and the field subsequently developed more rapidly than forecast, the specifications achieved for the optical system sufficiently exceeded the original goals that the resulting technology was still at the leading edge when it appeared.

The report also makes use of data on patenting output from the project. Over the six-year period, a total of 490 patents were filed, with a further 38 pending. In addition, figures are given for the number of research reports produced—out of the total of 1,789, ETL was responsible for 497 and the private sector 1,292. The reports are classified by field—for example, 'total system', 'component technology' and 'opto-electronic integrated-circuit technology.'

Finally, concerning industrial impact, the report notes that a significant amount of the technology developed in the project has already been implemented and that products will soon be introduced to the market. Most importantly, the participating firms were in the process of setting up a new joint-venture company to produce opto-electronic integrated-circuits. This began trading in September 1987 with launch-aid from the recently established AIST Key Technology Centre. Many of the staff were recruited from the laboratory set up during the project to undertake research on integrated optics.

AIST Laboratories

Outline of Mission

The sixteen AIST research institutes accounted in 1986 for just over 35 per cent of the Agency's total R&D expenditure of $820 million. The laboratories covered in this study—the National Research Laboratory of Metrology (NRLM), the Mechanical Engineering Laboratory (MEL), the National Chemical Laboratory for Industry (NCLI) and the Electrotechnical Laboratory (ETL)—have responsibility for developing a national capacity in many of the strategically important industrial technologies of the future. They include three of the five largest laboratories (see Figure 6) and have annual operating budgets ranging from $60 million (ETL) down to $14 million (NRLM). A brief description of the research undertaken in each institute is given in Figure 8.

In line with AIST policy, institutes have been encouraged, particularly since 1984, to move into more 'basic' lines of technological research. This is reflected in the Agency's current definition of the mission of its laboratories: 'at the research laboratories of AIST, work is carried out in developing the *leading* and *basic* technologies that will

The **Electrotechnical Laboratory (ETL)**, established in 1891, is Japan's largest national research organization specializing in electricity and electronics. The fields it covers include (1) fundamental electronic technology (solid state physics, electronic materials and devices, laser technology and three-dimensional IC technology); (2) information and computer technology (pattern recognition, computer architecture, software engineering and intelligent robots); (3) energy technology (solar energy, fuel cells and redox flow batteries, magnetic and laser nuclear fusion, superconductor applications, ocean thermal energy conversion and magnetohydrodynamic power generation) and (4) standards and measurements technology (establishment and supply of national standards for electricity, photometry, acoustics and ionizing radiation and radioactivity, and associated measurement technology). It is also active in such fields as biocybernetics, space electronics and pollution prevention.

Eelectrotechnical Laboratory	Tsukuba Gakuen 0298 (54) 5006
1-4, Umezono 1-chome, Sakura-mura, Niihari-gun, Ibaraki, 305	Research Planning Office

The **National Research Laboratory of Metrology (NRLM)** was established in 1903. Today it plays the leading role in unifying units and standards for the physical sciences and engineering Japan. For this purpose, it maintains close contact with the International Bureau of Weights and Measures, the International Organization of Legal Metrology and related institutions in the major industrialized countries.

NRLM's activities include the establishment and maintenance of standards and the development of precision measurement methods and apparatus for industrial applications. The Laboratory determines fundamental constants and evaluates mechanical and thermophysical properties of solid materials and fluids. Its responsibilities also extend to the calibration and testing of working standards and measurement instruments in compliance with the Measurement Law.

National Research Laboratory of Metrology	Tsukuba Gakuen 0298 (54) 4118
1-4, Umezono 1-chome, Sakura-mura, Niihari-gun, Ibaraki, 305	Senior Officer for Research Planning

The **Mechanical Engineering Laboratory (MEL)** was established in 1937 with the objective of encouraging Japan's machinery industry. Today MEL not only works with basic technology but also undertakes R&D on key frontier techniques which may involve high risks, and is expanding its activities aimed at promoting social development through the sophistication and systematization of mechanical engineering technology. In accordance with the demands of national policy and the laboratory's own specialties, R&D at MEL covers fields which include (1) the development and efficient utilization of resources and energy, (2) the application of new materials to machine elements and structures, (3) R&D on advanced robotics and (4) the development of technology for production, social welfare, industrial standards and international research cooperation.

Mechanical Engineering Laboratory	Tsukuba Gakuen 0298 (54) 2521
2, Namiki 1-chome, Sakura-mura, Niihari-gun, Ibaraki, 305	Research Planning Office

The **National Chemical Laboratory for Industry (NCLI)** was established in 1900 to develop technologies required in Japan's chemical industry. NCLI performs a broad range of basic and applied research on three basic types of technology: (1) technology for standardization and safety, including testing methods for standardization, a data bank on the physical properties of materials, safety assessment of explosives, and prevention of hazards caused by high pressure gases; (2) energy and resources technologies, including coal liquefaction, transportation of hydrogen by metal hydrides, a new aluminum production process using blast furnaces, a super heat pump energy accumulation system, and C_1-chemistry, biomass technology, and (3) basic technology for the chemical industry, including biotechnology, development of methods for catalyzing and synthesizing fine chemicals, and laser-introduced chemical reactions.

National Chemical Laboratory for Industry	Tsukuba Gakuen 0298 (54) 4431
1, Higashi 1-chome, Yatabe-machi, Tsukuba-gun, Ibaraki, 305	Research Planning Office

Figure 8 Summary of research activities of AIST institutes

Source: AIST (1986a, pp. 30–1)

form the *groundwork* for future technological innovations' (AIST 1986a, p. 29, emphasis added). Research undertaken by institutes is seen by AIST as having the following characteristics:

(a) research and development of leading technologies likely to form the basis of future technological innovation;
(b) research relating to the establishment and maintenance of technical standards (including the development of testing facilities);
(c) research addressing social needs, especially in earthquake prediction and environmental protection;
(d) fundamental experimental research beyond the resources of the private sector (AIST 1986a, p. 29).

The mechanisms for financing AIST laboratories are complex and require some explanation since they are closely related to the procedures used to evaluate research. There are three main types of support:

(a) 'ordinary R&D' — this covers personnel costs and core funding allocated on a per-capita basis ($9,000 per annum in 1987);
(b) 'special R&D' — this covers new capital investment, operating costs of central facilities, and funding for priority research on nuclear energy and the environment as well as research programmes agreed with AIST relating to the main missions of laboratories;
(c) 'designated R&D' — this is separately budgeted research financed through collaborative AIST initiatives such as the Large-Scale Programme, and grants and contracts obtained from other government organizations (such as the Science and Technology Agency).

The three support mechanisms fulfil different functions. 'Ordinary funds' are intended to provide a means by which institute staff, either individually or in groups, can carry out their preferred lines of research without external restrictions. They are thus seen as an investment in seedcorn ideas for the major new laboratory programmes of the future. 'Special funds', in contrast, are used by AIST to support the core activities essential for fulfilling each laboratory's mission. A portfolio of projects and programmes is agreed annually with each director, most institutes selecting a proportion of those sent for approval to AIST on the basis of competitive internal review of proposals. Finally, 'designated funds' are used as a mechanism to ensure that laboratories collaborate with industry, the academic community and other institutes in nationally agreed priority areas of research. Participation in such collaborative research (for example, within the Basic Technology for Future Industries Programme) is by far and away the most important avenue for technology transfer to industry. This mechanism for diffusing technology is much preferred by AIST over the alternative of allowing institutes to undertake contract work for industry which yields direct benefits to only one company. The intention is that laboratories should, as far as is possible, play a role in upgrading the technological capacity of Japanese industry as a whole.[7]

Although the AIST institutes include some of the world's leading research centres (the Electrotechnical Laboratory, most notably, is pre-eminent within its field), there have nevertheless been problems with organizational rigidity and ageing. These were partly solved by the substantial restructuring which took place when most of the laboratories moved in the late 1970s from Tokyo to their present site in Tsukuba Science City. However, the main means of revitalizing research activities has been to hold constant or even decrease the proportion of institute budgets coming in the form of 'ordinary' and 'special' funds, and to encourage greater competition for the 'designated' collaborative projects which have helped promote better links with industry. As a result, the more successful of the laboratories now have budget profiles in which expenditure on personnel and 'ordinary research' accounts for only 50 per cent of funding, while in others the figure is still over 70 per cent.

Approach to research evaluation

The issue of research evaluation was seen as important within all four laboratories. This stems from the realization that they will in future have to demonstrate greater accountability for the use of research funds both to the Administrative Inspection Bureau (which was in the process of reviewing NRLM) and to AIST (which, like other agencies, has been requested to evaluate its institutes by 1989 — see Management and Co-ordination Agency, 1984).

The interviews with senior laboratory staff revealed that the only systematic evaluation of research undertaken is conducted by AIST (and other ministries) in connection with the 'designated R&D' projects they support. Little or no ex-post assessment is carried out either internally or by AIST of 'ordinary' and 'special' research.

As one laboratory official remarked, 'generally speaking, we do not evaluate the success or failure of projects. We focus mainly on the evaluation of projects before they are set up, and, of course, we check the progress of research'.

In contrast to this lack of ex-post evaluation, much emphasis is placed by laboratories on routine monitoring and collection of data on individual projects and researchers. The standard procedure is that record cards are kept on all ongoing projects and the personal details and activities of research staff. Each institute usually has a senior planning officer whose duties include administering these records. In the case of NRLM, the details recorded on current projects are as follows:

(a) title of project;
(b) research group;
(c) principal investigator;
(d) duration;
(e) long-range targets (both technical and industrial — e.g. advancement of measurement techniques of thermal conductivity and viscosity of fluids, or review of viscosity standards and improvement of system of information transfer to industry);
(f) participating researchers;
(g) type of funding ('ordinary', 'special', 'designated');
(h) source of funding and cost of project;
(i) themes of planned research for each fiscal year;
(j) detailed plan of research with technical specifications for all component 'sub-projects', and names of researchers responsible;
(k) details of progress achieved over six-month periods in each sub-project — records are kept on a monthly basis and include details of recent work and new results, external collaboration, presentations at conferences, consultancy for companies, content of publications and patents;
(l) overall list of publications and presentations in each sub-project classified by author, subject and date.

The records kept on researchers follow a similar format but are more detailed. Each 'identity card' contains the following information:

(a) name and personal details of researcher;
(b) educational history;
(c) detailed description of research activities;

(d) listing of research output broken down by:
- articles in international scientific journals (English and Japanese)
- other published research articles
- review papers in journals
- published conference proceedings
- oral presentations at conferences
- published reports of the laboratory
- lectures at private or semi-official meetings
- advice and consultancy for industry
- patents and other intellectual property
- prizes received.

Such data are mainly used in the annual review of staff performance and research activity[8] carried out by the laboratory director in preparing the budget submission to AIST. At this time, formal decisions are taken on staff promotion and selection of projects for both the 'ordinary' and 'special' programmes.

Although not currently used for this purpose, the information on research staff and projects is sufficiently comprehensive to form the basis of a systematic post-performance review system. However, those interviewed felt that strong barriers exist in most institutes against introducing assessment of this sort since it would result in public judgements being made about the 'success' or 'failure' of both individuals and research groups. This is not currently culturally acceptable except in institutes like ETL which receive larger numbers of foreign visitors and have a more internationalist perspective, and explains why external peer-review of the type common in Western countries is rarely used in Japanese laboratories.

Officials interviewed also expressed worries about the external pressures on laboratories to adopt an overly mechanistic approach to research evaluation. They felt that researchers would quickly learn to 'play' the system by producing, for example, large numbers of routine papers and patent applications at the expense of more creative work. This, it was argued, was a possible danger with the *Guidelines for Research Evaluation* (CST 1986b) (discussed in Chapter 2).

Despite these reservations, there was widespread acceptance that more systematic evaluation, especially of 'ordinary' research, would improve efficiency in laboratories and act as a stimulus to terminating long-running projects making little contribution to meeting national technological needs. However, any evaluation system instituted needs to take as its starting point the mission of AIST laboratories which is to develop 'fundamental technologies' capable of creating the 'seeds for new generations of industrial products'. The ETL official felt that, to discharge its mission successfully, his laboratory had to 'lead industry by two or three steps'. If the time for commercializing products is included, this means that any quantitative evaluation of ETL's research performance will necessarily have to be carried out on a long-term basis, in some cases up to five years after completion of a programme. The laboratory has just undertaken an internal review of its evaluation system (ETL, 1986), and has decided not to adopt the CST proposals. The best way of judging the impact and likely future benefits from ETL work, it was argued, is through surveys of relevant industrial companies. This view was shared by the officials interviewed in the other laboratories.

Notes

1. This is undertaken by the Japan Industrial Technology Association (JITA), a non-profit foundation with the role of diffusing the technical achievements of AIST-funded work in an effective manner. JITA holds the patent rights to the results of AIST research and cooperates with the Research Development Corporation of Japan (JRDC) to promote their commercial utilization by industry — see AIST (1986a, p. 25) and JRDC (1986).
2. A more detailed description of the AIST Large-Scale R&D Programme and the procedures employed in evaluating projects is given in Tanaka (1987).
3. Tanaka (*op. cit.*, p. 16) stresses the central role of the project officer in routine monitoring of progress: 'The manager also conducts an annual check and reviews the process of fixing the yearly base-budgets. He and his staff, normally three or four people, should have a bird's-eye view of the project and be especially sensitive to changes in the situation of overall R&D activities so as not to lose sight of the social and economic demands within the field of the project. He interviews and contacts parties related to the project and participates in seminars and conferences about the project. Implicitly, he is always in the process of evaluating the project, through close contact with the promoting bodies, private firms and national research institutes.'
4. According to Tanaka (*op. cit.*, p. 19), the assessment manual currently used lists five very general evaluation criteria: (a) the extent to which the research will achieve the objectives set out in the basic plan; (b) the results of the research, especially in comparison with technical levels abroad; (c) its impact on other fields and the extent to which the results

are utilized; (d) appropriateness of the basic plan including objectives, methods and budgetary proposals; and (e) appropriateness of the measures and processes to achieve the objectives set out in the basic plan.
5. The patent which has generated most royalty income to date concerns the 'desalination of seawater.' Total revenue over the last ten years has been around $1 million—see AIST (1986a, p. 25).
6. According to the AIST official responsible for this project, the decision to terminate work one year early was not the result of a formal evaluation of progress. Rather, it was taken by means of informal consensus-based discussions between himself, participants in the project, and the Assessment Subcommittee.
7. This is not to suggest that institutes do not work with individual companies. On the contrary, linkages are extremely wide-ranging and are both of a formal and informal nature. ETL, for example, typically has 200–300 visiting scientists from industry working within its laboratories each year, as well as providing assistance on standards, testing, sample materials and routine technical advice.
8. This is known as the 'Director-General's Hearing'. The procedure by which it is carried out in AIST laboratories is described in detail in Nagasu (1983). The article also outlines the general approach to R&D evaluation employed within the National Aerospace Laboratory.

4
Evaluation of Applied Research by the Science and Technology Agency

Structure and Organization of STA

The Science and Technology Agency (STA) has the dual role of co-ordinating overall national scientific and technological activities and funding research in areas not covered by other government departments—that is, in nuclear energy, aviation, space, ocean development and natural resources. The responsibilities of STA are as follows:

(a) formulation, implementation and co-ordination of basic science and technology policies;
(b) administration of the 'Special Co-ordination Funds for Science and Technology' which come under the aegis of the Council for Science and Technology;
(c) funding the programme on 'Exploratory Research for Advanced Technology' (ERATO);
(d) operating a network of six national laboratories and seven 'public research corporations';
(e) strengthening the foundations of the nation's infrastructure for science and technology;
(f) promoting international co-operation in science and technology (STA, 1985b, p. 1).

Details of the Agency's research activities and its 1985 budget of $2.8 billion are given in Table 6.

As with AIST, the diversity of STA's activities meant that the study had to be highly selective in the areas of research covered. Those chosen were the two research programmes (Special Co-ordination Funds for Science and Technology and ERATO) and three institutes (the National Institute for Research in Inorganic Materials, the National Research Institute for Metals, and the Institute of Physical and Chemical Research). The major energy, aerospace and environmental institutes operated by STA were excluded from consideration in order to focus on the more general areas of industrial technology.

Table 6 Research activities and budget of Science and Technology Agency fiscal year 1985 (millions of yen)

Items		Budget for FY 1984 (A)	Budget for FY 1985 (B)	Increase (B − A)	Ratio over previous year (B/A)
I.	General Account	*109,006 329,346	*93,090 329,529	*−15,916 183	100.1%
II.	Special Account for Industrial Investment	—	2,900	2,900	—
	(Subtotal)	*109,006 329,346	*93,090 332,429	*−15,916 3,083	100.9%
III.	Special Account for Power Source Development	*76,535 78,745	*89,168 88,478	*12,633 9,733	112.4%
	(1) Account for Siting Power Plants and Other Atomic Energy Facilities	10,481	12,124	1,643	115.7%
	(2) Account for Diversification of Power Sources	*76,535 68,264	*89,168 76,354	*12,633 8,090	111.9%
	Total	*185,541 408,091	*182,258 420,907	*−3,283 12,816	103.1%

I. General Account and Special Account for Industrial Investment

Items		Budget for FY 1984 (A)	Budget for FY 1985 (B)	Increase (B − A)
1.	Strengthening Planning and Coordination Functions in Science and Technology Administration	6,530	7,330	800
	(1) Special Coordination Funds for Promoting Science and Technology	6,300	7,100	800
	(2) Planning and Coordination by the Council for Science and Technology and Other Organs	230	230	0
2.	Support for Foundations for Promoting Science and Technology	4,739	5,198	459
	(1) Information Exchange in Science and Technology	4,205	4,666	461
	General Account	4,205	1,768	−2,439
	Special Account for Industrial Investment	—	2,900	2,900
	(2) Promotion of Exchange of Researchers and Other Items	534	532	−2
3.	Promotion of International Cooperation in the fields of Science and Technology	*2,976 5,259	*3,345 6,594	*369 1,335
	Strengthening and Widening of International Personal Exchange (including above)	(926)	(1,164)	(238)
4.	Advancing National Understanding of Science and Technology	*5,619 26,894	9,412	*−5,619 −17,482
	(1) The International Exposition of Science and Technology	*5,619 26,703	9,241	*−5,619 −17,462
	(2) Public Relations Activities in Science and Technology	191	171	−20
5.	Promotion of Research and Development in priority fields of Science and Technology	*103,387 288,112	*93,090 307,313	*−10,297 19,201
	(1) Promotion of Creative Science and Technology by Flexible Research Systems	2,296	2,570	274
	(2) Promotion of Atomic Energy Research, Development and Utilization	*46,101 166,112	*41,614 178,020	*−4,487 11,908
	(a) Administration of nuclear safety regulation and environmental Safety Measures	2,046	2,054	8

* Government guarantee of appropriation for future R&D

Table 6 — cont.

Items	Budget for FY 1984 (A)	Budget for FY 1985 (B)	Increase (B − A)
(b) Power Reactor and Nuclear Fuel Development Corporation	*10,556 63,702	*9,780 65,769	*−776 2,067
(c) Japan Atomic Energy Research Institute	*31,808 90,319	*30,704 99,674 *345	*−1,104 9,355 *345
(d) National Institute of Radiological Science	6,052	5,551	−501
(e) Research at National Research Institutes	1,732	1,733	1
(f) Research at Institute of Physical and Chemical Research	*3,737 1,516	*785 2,545	*−2,952 1,029
(3) Promotion of Space Development	*55,401 85,812	*48,818 91,585	*−6,583 5,773
(a) National Space Development Agency of Japan	*54,327 84,358	*48,818 88,861	*−5,509 4,503
(b) Research on space development at National Aerospace Laboratory	*1,074 918	— 2,197	*−1,074 1,279
(4) Promotion of Ocean Development	5,146	6,875	1,729
(a) Japan Marine Science and Technology Centre	4,963	6,700	1,737
(b) Other Ocean Development Projects	183	175	−8
(5) Promotion of Life Science	[*604] [7,657]	[*611] [8,456]	[*7] [799]
(6) Research and Development of Materials Technology	7,507	7,810	303
(7) Promotion of Important Integrated Research	*1,885 21,239	*2,658 20,453 *203	*773 −786 *203
(a) Promotion of Disaster Prevention Science and Technology	2,109 *1,281	2,091 *1,844	−18 *563
(b) Promotion of Research and Development of Aviation Technology at National Aerospace Laboratory	8,863	7,813	−1,050
(c) Other Research	*604 10,267	*611 10,549	*7 282

II. Special Account for Power Sources Development

Items	Budget for FY 1984 (A)	Budget for FY 1985 (B)	Increase (B − A)
Account for Siting Power Plants and Other Atomic Energy Facilities	10,481	12,124	1,643
1. Commission Funds for Nuclear Power Safety Measures, etc.	4,533	4,738	205
2. Power Plant Siting Promotion Subsidy	2,507	3,659	1,152
3. Special Subsidies for Power Plant Siting	1,300	1,319	19
4. Subsidies for Nuclear Power Safety Measures, etc.	2,023	2,293	270
Account for Diversification of Power Sources	*76,535 68,264	*89,168 76,354	*12,633 8,090
1. Power Reactor and Nuclear Fuel Development Corporation	*76,535 63,963	*89,168 72,013	*12,633 8,050
(1) Development of Advanced Power Reactor	*53,107 33,315	*86,112 45,232	*33,005 11,917
(2) Development of Technology for Reprocessing of Spent Fuel	*3,825 22,490	*2,719 16,221	*−1,106 −6,269
(3) Development of Uranium Enrichment Technology	*19,603 8,158	*336 10,560	*−19,267 2,402
2. Other Expenditure	4,301	4,341	40
Total	*76,535 78,745	*89,168 88,478	*12,633 9,733

Special Co-ordination Funds for Science and Technology

Outline of Programme

The 'Special Co-ordination Funds' programme was initiated in 1981 to fill the 'gaps' between research supported by the different government agencies and ministries, especially in areas identified as requiring an urgent and flexible inter-departmental response. Annual expenditure on the programme has risen from $22 million in 1981 to $53 million in 1986 (CST, 1986c, p. 21). Funds are distributed by STA in line with recommendations made by the Council for Science and Technology through its three subcommittees on Basic Research, Research Survey and Research Evaluation (see Chapter 2, notes 1 and 10). The main criteria for selection of projects are as follows:

(a) promotion of pioneering and fundamental research;
(b) promotion of research and development requiring co-operation among several organizations;
(c) reinforcement of systematic co-operation between industry, government and universities;
(d) flexible response to any emerging research requirement to meet urgent needs;
(e) promotion of international collaboration; and
(f) implementation of research evaluation and analysis of R&D (STA, 1985, p. 2).

Current projects are primarily in areas of longer-term strategic research where an interdisciplinary perspective is required. The broad fields covered include materials science, life sciences, anti-gravity, information technology and earth science. The duration of projects varies but is normally five years.

Approach to Evaluation

The CST Subcommittee on Research Evaluation has overall responsibility for assessment. It appoints a working group for each project which incudes four or five experts in the field drawn from universities, institutes and industry. Given that the Subcommittee itself helped draft the *Guidelines for Research Evaluation* (discussed in Chapter 2), it is not surprising that the Special Co-ordination Funds programme is the first case where the proposals have been fully implemented within government.

According to the STA official responsible for servicing the Evaluation Subcommittee, the most important phase of assessment is at the beginning of projects when the technical goals are set. At this 'pre-evaluation' stage, a project structure is established comprising 'main-frame' activities, component sub-projects, and detailed research themes within each sub-project.

Formal evaluation is undertaken at the mid-term stage of projects, generally three years into the research, as well as at the end on receipt of the final report. Because projects are often interdisciplinary and differ significantly in their nature and aims, it has not been possible to develop a single set of criteria for assessing research performance. However, in all cases the research results achieved are compared carefully with the technical objectives set out in the original project plan.

The official interviewed strongly argued that evaluation should be linked to the management of research, and for this reason mid-term review is probably of greater value than ex-post assessment since it provides an opportunity to influence constructively the outcome of the work. In particular, the number of themes within sub-projects is often reduced after mid-term evaluation, enabling support for more successful lines of research to be increased. The overall budgets of sub-projects are also sometimes adjusted, as happened recently within a life-science project on ageing when funds for a very successful sub-project on Alzheimer's disease (which had within three years produced important results on the basic genetic mechanism involved) were significantly increased. This was at the expense of a sub-project on 'appropriate living environments' where funding was terminated.

It is a requirement that details of all publications and patent applications arising from projects are appended to mid-term and final reports. However, while review of publications, in particular, is taken into account in evaluation, the principal criterion is the extent to which the technical goals have been achieved. No attempt is made to estimate the likely industrial or other impacts of research results since even those with possible practical value are rarely anywhere near being implemented within the time-frame of the assessment process.

The STA official felt that the evaluation system was on balance working reasonably well, especially at the mid-term and final assessment stages. The main problem being encountered is that technical goals for research themes within sub-projects are not being specified in sufficient detail at the 'pre-evaluation' stage, but this is in the process of being remedied by implementing the assessment procedures described in Chapter 2. He also thought the working group' concept was proving satisfactory and that assistance from outside evaluators was probably unnecessary. Although this might improve 'objectivity', it would limit the extent to which working group members would be able to interact informally with researchers to steer projects experiencing problems in the required direction. As in most other government programmes, the role of consensus-based routine monitoring and review is clearly significant.

Exploratory Research for Advanced Technology (ERATO)

Outline of Programme

The ERATO programme was established in 1981 as an experiment to develop creative strategic science capable of 'sowing the seeds which pave avenues for developing innovative technologies' (STA, 1985b, p. 3). By then, the Japanese government had realized that the same factors which previously had led to the nation's unprecedented industrial successes were likely to limit progress in the future as fundamental science and technology became increasingly important. Shogo Kurachi, formerly President of the Research Development Corporation of Japan (JRDC), which has direct responsibility for administering the programme, stated the problem as follows:

Most technologies available in Japan have been borrowed so far, and very few technologies have been created or developed here. The question is, why are Japanese, who have completely mastered and advanced the mass production technology, unable to generate new technological ideas which can serve to drive technological innovations?

We have analyzed this problem from various perspectives, and have come to the conclusion that the various factors which contributed to the realization of efficient mass production technology are, at the same time, hindering the development of radically new technologies by the Japanese . . . People in a group in Japan follow its leader. Group orientedness is an invisible but gigantic pillar which supports Japanese industries.

On the other hand, in such a society independent action by a member of a group is looked at with disfavour. Therefore, if a person comes up with a creative idea and wishes to realize it, he is not likely to be rewarded for his action. He may even be driven out of the group as an alien element. In such a society, creative ideas are hard to be recognized and realized. Thus if radically new technologies are to be developed in Japan, it is necessary to organize a new group dedicated to the creation of new technologies outside of the already existing groups. Members of the new group are encouraged to engage in research as freely as possible (Kurachi nd, pp. 1-2).

The structure of the ERATO programme is outlined in Figure 9. Eight projects are currently being supported, each running for five years at an average cost of nearly $13 million. The underlying theme of most projects is the physical, chemical and biological properties of new materials. The way the programme is organized differs from the normal model of government-funded research in several respects:

(a) talented leaders (project directors) are vested with considerable management responsibility once a research plan has been agreed;
(b) the project director recruits gifted researchers from industry, universities and government laboratories to conduct research under a system in which individual talents and creativity are utilized to the full. Preference is given to researchers under thirty-five years old, and the normal restrictions on recruiting foreign scientists have been lifted;
(c) projects are managed flexibly, with objectives changed when necessary depending on progress;
(d) research is undertaken principally in private sector laboratories and facilities. These are rented for five years after which the temporary project laboratory is closed (STA, 1985b, p. 3).

Care has been taken to ensure that the system for protecting industrial property rights encourages participation by companies. Patents are owned jointly by JRDC and the individual inventor(s) who, if from industry, can transfer the rights to their employer on completion of the project. Although initially suspicious of allowing rented laboratory space to be open to outsider scientists (and indeed some firms have excluded researchers from direct competitors), companies are increasingly welcoming the initiative and seconding their better young scientists. At present sixty per cent of researchers in the programme come from industry.

Evaluation of Programme

While most government research programmes emphasize the setting of detailed and verifiable technical goals, the key task in ERATO has been to select project directors capable of managing unorthodox and

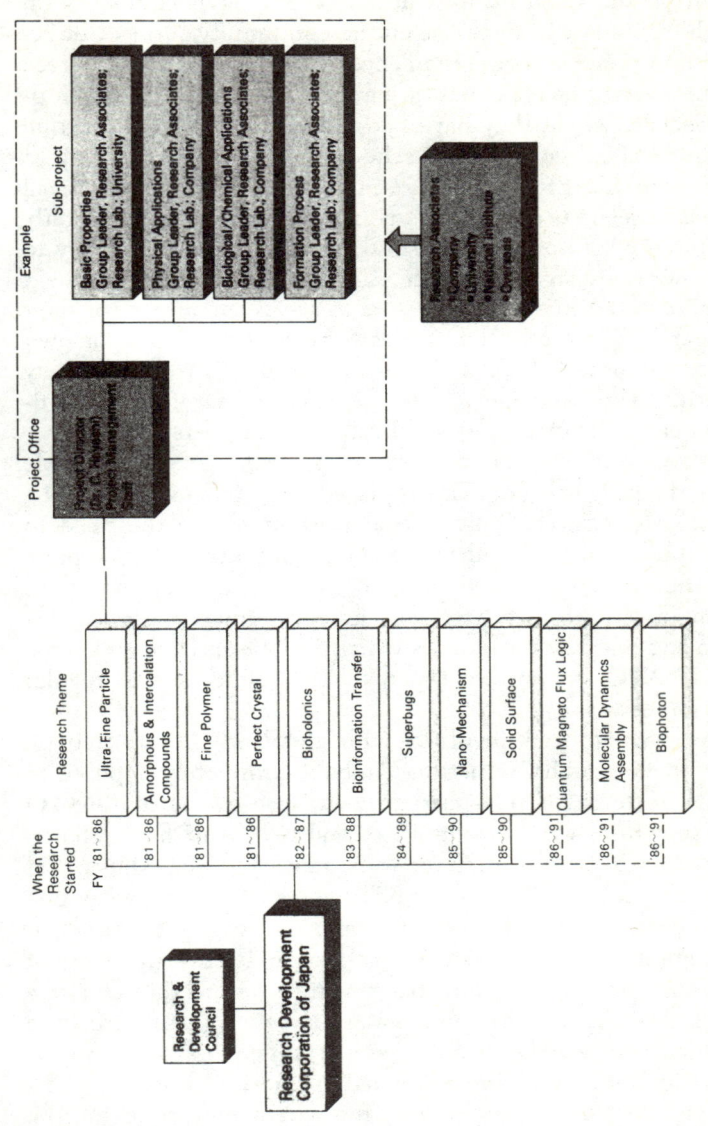

Figure 9 Outline of Exploratory Research for Advanced Technology Programme (ERATO)

uncertain research. Possible research themes are identified through surveys of technological trends conducted by consultants (for example, from the Institute for Future Technology), coupled with informal discussions within the scientific community. Project directors with appropriate skills are then chosen on the basis of their track record in pioneering radically new scientific or technological developments, especially where they have had to overcome critical reaction from an entrenched, conservative school of thought.[1] According to the Director of the ERATO programme, Genya Chiba, the usual procedure is to select three candidate directors who are then 'secretly checked to see what young scientists think of their work. We try to find out whose research approach is being endorsed by the next generation.' Citation data are also used to assess the impact of their recent research. Once selected, project directors develop their own research programme which specifies the goals only in relatively general terms. They are then given assistance in recruiting a multi-disciplinary cadre of young, 'pre-established' researchers.

Chiba stressed that project directors are allowed considerable freedom, and hence little emphasis is placed on systematic monitoring of research progress. The only formal restrictions are the need to operate within an agreed budget, to submit interim annual reports outlining the results achieved, and to produce a final report on completion of the project. Stress is, however, placed on the dissemination and discussion of results which are presented at an annual three-day ERATO symposium (open to the public) and at regular professional meetings.

Although having been involved with the CST Committee on Guidelines for Research Evaluation, Chiba is completely opposed to any traditional form of mid-term or final assessment of ERATO projects. He refuses even to allow external review of final reports. Such a position is proving difficult to sustain, with the Ministry of Finance putting political pressure on STA who are in turn pressurizing JRDC. The reasons why Chiba is, as he put it, 'begging them not to force evaluation in the near future' relate to the long-term nature of the programme and his concern that this may be the thin end of a wedge of orthodoxy which could undermine the creative freedom now accorded to researchers. While not in principle against evaluation, Chiba feels it should not be carried out until at least five years after the end of ERATO projects. This would give time for the research results to diffuse and the industrial benefits to become visible. The main criterion he would wish to see applied in assessment is the 'technological fundamentality' of the research—that is, whether it has succeeded in creating the basis for new families of industrial products or processes. In his view, only industrialists are in a position to make judgements of this type, although quantitative indicators such as patent royalties and investment by firms in new technology can be useful.

Chiba argues that post-hoc review by technical experts carried out immediately on completion of projects (of the sort conducted by AIST in the Basic Technology for Future Industries Programme) could be misleading or even dangerous. He does not

> trust a committee of academic scientists to evaluate the results of technologically oriented research. Whether industry invests in the new technology created is the crucial test. So I am saying to the government, 'please wait'. If they force me, we can form an evaluation committee of established scientists for a ceremony. The question, though, is whether what they say is trustworthy, and from my experience premature review often results in big mistakes being made. In addition, fundamental progress in science and technology is essentially made by the younger generation, and it is made by throwing away and replacing the work of the older generation. The average age of evaluation committees is normally 55–65—they are the outgoing generation. If you are old, informed and wise you cannot make breakthroughs nor, often, can you recognize them. The established generation should not restrict the new generation by conservatively evaluating their work. I have been a victim of such committees—the conclusions they reach are normally the commonsense summing up of that age-group's experience. There are exceptions, but this is the rule [Interview, February 1987].

This said, Chiba does recognize the value of the traditional consensus-seeking approach to R&D management in the case of applied research where the technical aims can be relatively clearly specified. However, his programme aims to demonstrate that Japanese researchers can, given the right environment, produce paradigm-changing creative basic technology. Since pressures to social conformity are exercised through the evaluation system, he had no option other than to take a stand against the introduction of formal assessment.

Despite Chiba's resistance to immediate evaluation of the four ERATO projects recently completed, it could seem unlikely that *any* review committee, however constituted, would assess the programme negatively. In the period 1981–6, 800 scientific papers were published[2] (30 per cent in foreign journals) and 380 patents were filed. Moreover, licences have already been granted (in February 1987) for three patents from the Perfect Crystal Project, while a patent from the Fine Polymer Project has generated requests from no less than 160 US companies to purchase the rights. According to Chiba, 'three of the first four projects have produced major breakthroughs which will lead to new product areas or technologies'. For example, in the Perfect Crystal Project work on molecular-level devices has made possible a new generation of large-scale integrated circuits (LSIs), while the Ultra-Fine Particle Project has yielded results on catalysis which will also be useful for the production of LSIs.

Finally, an evaluation committee for ERATO would have to take into account its novel organizational workings[3] and the flexibility to open and close laboratories without having to be concerned about infrastructural investments. In the case of the four completed projects, all 100 researchers have either returned to their seconding organizations (mostly industrial companies) or are working elsewhere.

Research Institutes Administered by STA

Mission of Institutes

The missions of the national laboratories and public research corporations coming under the aegis of the Science and Technology Agency range from high-technology development activities, such as those carried out by the National Space Development Agency (NASDA) and the National Aerospace Laboratory (NAL), to longer-term basic research (see STA, 1985b).

The two in-house STA institutes covered in the study are primarily concerned with strategic research (which they term 'oriented basic research') but they also carry out some specific applied research. The first, the National Research Institute for Metals (NRIM), works on materials development and reliability, and process engineering. It also operates large metallurgical testing facilities for creep and fatigue (see NRIM, 1985). The second, the National Institute for Research in Inorganic Materials (NIRIM), specializes in the study of ultra-high purity compounds, carrying out research on chemical synthesis, analysis of chemical composition and structures, and evaluation of properties of materials (see NIRIM, 1986).

The Institute of Physical and Chemical Research (RIKEN), which has the status of a 'Public Research Corporation', was also included in the study. Although it undertakes some strategic research and to a lesser extent applied research, many of its activities are fundamental in nature and not dissimilar to the work of a university. Its programme is wide-ranging and includes research on geosciences, biological engineering, enzymes and design of catalysts, laser science, solar energy, agricultural chemicals, medical science, molecular genetics and molecular oncology (see Institute of Physical and Chemical Research, 1986). RIKEN is by far the largest of the institutes, with a budget of around $80 million in 1986, compared with $12 million and $28 million for NIRIM and NRIM. Although financed by STA, the method of reearch support is broadly similar to that for AIST laboratories described in Chapter 3 and is not therefore discussed further here.

Approach to Evaluation

The nature and extent of evaluation activities in the three institutes generally parallel those in AIST laboratories, and can be summarized as follows:

(a) the emphasis is on routine monitoring and collection of data on research staff (their publications, conference presentations, patents, etc.). This information is used mainly as an input to the annual 'Director-General's Hearing';
(b) little or no evaluation is carried out of the output from either 'ordinary research' or 'special research' (coming within the 'ordinary budget' of STA);
(c) the only systematic mid-term or post-hoc assessment relates to the 'designated' and other earmarked research supported, for example, through Special Co-ordination Funds or the Basic Technology for Future Industries Programme;
(d) research management has focused on the definition and selection of new projects and programmes rather than on evaluation of present or past ones.

Besides these general points, a few detailed observations are worth making. First, the Science and Technology Agency has been encouraging institutes to develop internal evaluation systems, and this has led to discussions on how to measure research performance. Apart from specific applied research where one can assess the extent to which technical objectives have been realized, institutes reported problems in conceiving how they might measure the success and impact of their work. This was a particular problem, for example, with the NRIM metallurgical testing facilities (for creep and fatigue) where the tangible outputs are data sheets, irregular tests and sample materials. Contract income cannot be used to evaluate such activities since the policy is to provide most services free to government and industry.

Second, NRIM argued that evaluation alone is insufficient for achieving 'value for money' in research. The official interviewed felt that government institutes were often bureaucratic and resistant to change. NIRIM had attempted to avoid such problems by instituting a system whereby, instead of the traditional divisional structure, staff were divided into fifteen research groups. These are formed for five years only and, unless there are strong reasons for continuing, are then dissolved and new groups with different research themes established. In around ten per cent of cases, a new group leader will also be appointed by the director. This has the disadvantage that it can lead to personal problems for the deposed group head (one recently committed suicide), but the group system is felt by senior management to facilitate a more dynamic research programme, and is seen as largely responsible for the laboratory's above average scientific and technological output.[4] Since its establishment as an STA institute in 1966, 483 Japanese and forty-eight foreign patents have been filed by the 120 researchers at an annual rate of 0.5 per staff member. Of these, forty-eight have been commercialized including one on 'potassium titanate fibres' which has yielded considerable royalties.[5]

Finally, reference should be make to RIKEN which, together with ETL, is probably the best known research institute internationally. Because of its long-standing participation in the world scientific community, some use is made of peer review which is not the case with most other Japanese laboratories. A distinctive feature of the evaluation system in place in the institute concerns the procedure for replacing retiring directors of the forty-five 'internal laboratories'. This begins with the Council of Laboratory Directors (CLD) setting up a review committee to investigate

(a) the achievements of the laboratory under the old director;
(b) the rationale for the laboratory's continued operation;
(c) the case for modifying its lines of research;
(d) whether it should be closed;
(e) the possibilities for creating a new laboratory;
(f) the availability of a replacement director.

The review committee is usually made up of five internal laboratory directors and Members of Council. There is no representation from outside RIKEN although the committee does seek the views of external experts and of course closely consults STA. After a year or so,[6] recommendations are made and a report submitted to the CLD for approval and then to the President of RIKEN for a final decision.

The review of laboratories following the retirement of directors is the main means by which RIKEN's research activities have been restructured. In recent years, the isotope laboratory and two oceanography laboratories have been closed. In their place, three new life-science laboratories have been established in line with government policy to strengthen Japanese strategic research in the area. Within ten years of the appointment of a new director, it is required that an external review be carried out of the research achievements of their laboratory. The review committee contains outside specialists drawn from universities, research institutes and companies. Given the increasing interest shown by companies in long-term strategic research, little difficulty is experienced in gaining their participation. The report produced by the review committee is submitted to the President and includes advice on the management of the laboratory (see Shibata, 1987).

Notes

1. For example, Chiba pointed to Junichi Nishizawa, head of the Perfect Crystal Project, whose discovery of the static induction transistor when he was twenty-three years old was never accepted in Japan. Similarly, Nishizawa proposed in 1964 an optical transmission system using quartz fibres and filed for a Japanese patent on the invention. This was turned down by the Patent Office for technical reasons. Five years later, Corning Glass filed for a similar patent which was subsequently awarded. As a result, Nishizawa failed to gain credit for pioneering fibre-optic communications. A legal suit is still under way in Japan alleging mistakes were made by the Patent Office and claiming priority for the invention.
2. It should be noted that there has been a qualitative improvement over recent years in Japan's relative international performance in basic research as judged by world shares in publications (a measure of output) and citations (which indicate scientific impact on the research community). This is particularly the case in the areas of basic materials and applied physical sciences research focused on in ERATO and the Basic Technology for Future Industries Programme. Publication and citation data for Japan relative to other major industrial nations are reported in Martin *et al.* (1987).

3. Chiba stressed that ERATO had in particular demonstrated the benefits of opening up the previously closed Japanese research system to visiting foreign scientists. Other government research programmes were now in the process of following suit and adopting this policy. It is also of note that the National Science Foundation will shortly be seconding one of its officials to JRDC for a few months to gain detailed experience of the workings of the ERATO programme, and to determine whether it would be feasible to develop a similar scheme in the US. There would be much to be gained if the UK also considered taking serious steps to learn from the highly novel R&D management structures employed in ERATO.
4. Among STA laboratories, the National Institute for Research in Inorganic Materials has an especially basic orientation. The continual restructuring of research groups can in some ways be regarded as an alternative solution to limiting the tendencies towards conservatism in the Japanese R&D system that Chiba is attempting to overcome in the ERATO programme.
5. The disadvantage of insisting on regular break-up of research groups is that mistakes can sometimes be made as happened in 1973 with the termination of the institute's work on zirconium. This line of research was subsequently to prove of importance to the laboratory's future work on high-performance ceramics, and an existing research group in the area would in all likelihood have played a valuable role.
6. Tanaka (1987, p. 9) points out that one of the main problems with consensus-seeking committee mechanisms is the length of time it takes to achieve decisions.

5
Evaluation of Applied Research by Companies

Interviews were conducted with five companies—Hitachi, Mitsubishi Electric Corporation, NEC Corporation, Sharp Corporation and Toray Industries—whose business activities are principally in the electronic and electrical engineering, materials engineering, chemical and biotechnology sectors. The aim was to establish which approaches and techniques are generally used within firms to evaluate strategic and applied research, and, more specifically, how the results of government-funded research are assessed.[1] Companies were also asked for their views on the overall adequacy of evaluation within government programmes and research institutes.

General Approach to Research Evaluation

Although differing in their organizational structures for planning, managing and executing R&D, all five firms employ broadly similar approaches to monitoring and assessing research. Longer-term strategic research and specific applied research are evaluated in rather different ways and it is therefore necessary to discuss these separately.

Longer-Term Strategic Research

In the companies visited, strategic research is generally carried out within central laboratories and is financed principally by corporate headquarters rather than by operating divisions. The officials interviewed reported that longer-term research has been growing rapidly in importance over recent years, and now accounts for between ten and thirty per cent of central research laboratory activities. The average duration of projects is five years, although they can extend to ten or even fifteen years.

Companies invest heavily in monitoring and forecasting scientific and technological trends, and therefore feel they have a reasonably clear idea as to what are likely to be the key research areas for the future and their potential impact on major business sectors.[2] For example, NEC has identified thirty core technology areas (for example, pattern recognition), and predicts for both the medium and long term how development of the underlying basic technologies (voice, character, figure, image and object recognition) will provide new manufacturing opportunties (in switching, transmission and terminals, radio, information processing, industrial systems and electronic devices). Strategic research projects, which have to promise a high degree of 'originality', generally fit within such a longer-term framework and are carried out by staff with an above-average record of creativity in basic research.

The extent to which technical goals are set when projects begin varies across companies and with the nature and duration of the planned research. Most often, goals are initially specified in relatively general terms and relate to novel functions or target operating levels within defined physical limits. The goals then become technically more specific as the project progresses.

Some companies also have a policy of predicting the commercial benefits that will accrue if project targets are realized. Although the success rates of such forecasts have so far been poor (the predictions have been unduly optimistic), the exercise is nevertheless seen as useful in terms of bringing home to researchers the fact that their work must ultimately be paid for by new and improved products or processes.

All five companies annually carry out formal evaluations of ongoing projects prior to renewing funding. This is normally undertaken by a Corporate R&D Planning Committee which typically is comprised of the President and Managing Director, the Directors of the Central Research Laboratory and Divisional Research Laboratories, and a number of senior staff from operating divisions. Annual review is coupled with a relatively flexible approach to monitoring progress on a day-to-day basis, with laboratory management requesting written reports every six months or so. In very long-term projects, major stage assessments are carried out only every two or three years. Where breakthroughs with possible commercial value are made, projects are then subject to closer and more frequent evaluation.

The criteria used routinely to assess progress in longer-term research projects usually hinge on evaluation of journal and conference papers which researchers are encouraged to publish, providing the data reported have first been screened for possible commercial sensitivity.[3] Later in a project, the number of patents and their importance to the firm takes on greater significance. More generally, research is evaluated in terms of whether logical progress has been made over the previous year in terms of techniques, method, measurement, and so on. Checklists are normally used in such assessments.

On completion of projects, the main criterion for evaluation is the 'fundamentality' of the research—that is, whether it has produced a novel invention or development, or significantly advanced the technology base of the company. Analysis of patents and their current or likely future utilization by the company was reported as being especially important here. Research papers are also evaluated as is the extent to which the original targets have been met. Finally, assessment is made in most cases of the likely commercial impact over the next three to five years of technology developed within the project, recognizing that the time-horizon for implementation is such that estimates are necessarily often inaccurate.

The impression given by those interviewed was that the procedures currently used by companies to evaluate longer-term research are not wholly satisfactory, and that improved methods are needed. The recent emphasis on increased funding for strategic applied research means that evaluation is becoming an important issue for corporate R&D management.

Specific Applied Research

Specific applied research is undertaken within both central research laboratories and operating divisions. Because it is often required as an input to development programmes, the procedures for initiating projects, routine monitoring of progress, and mid-term and ex-post evaluation are systematized to a much greater extent than is the case with longer-term strategic research.

Decisions to establish projects within a company's central research laboratory are usually made by the 'Corporate R&D Planning Committee' in close consultation with operating divisions. Projects initiated within divisional laboratories will generally be decided by an 'R&D Planning Committee' which has a somewhat wider membership, including representatives from sales and marketing. In both cases, the criteria for project selection include the following:

(a) relevance of the proposed technology to the company's development needs;
(b) competitiveness of the technology relative to alternatives;
(c) investment and personnel requirements compared with alternative R&D possibilities (i.e. the opportunity costs of investment);
(d) likely return on investment if the technical goals set for the project are achieved (these are often estimated for three, five, and sometimes ten years into the future);
(e) technical competence of the company to undertake the project and availability of researchers with suitable expertise;
(f) level of technical uncertainty;
(g) potential impact on other technology areas;
(h) other by-products and externalities (one company uses a list of eight types of potential spin-off).

The length of projects varies between six months and five years, the average being around two years. Firms usually classify projects according to their relative importance (for example, 'vitally important', 'very important', 'important', and 'of interest') and this determines the extent of monitoring and the seniority of staff involved. In the case of extremely urgent research, monthly checks on progress may be carried out by corporate executives, while responsibility for monitoring other projects is generally left to section heads or laboratory management.

All the companies reported that projects are assessed regularly (typically every six months) by laboratory directors, with a more formal review being undertaken annually by an Evaluation Committee. This tends to have a membership similar to the R&D Planning Committee, although in some companies both functions are performed by the same committee.

During annual and mid-term review, account is taken of patents and publications (which are often compared with those of competitor companies), whether predicted 'technical milestones' are being achieved, whether expenditure is in line with the planned budget, and the extent to which the technology remains competitive in the marketplace. Revisions are also normally made to the calculations of expected return on investment if the research is successful.

The procedures used in the final evaluation of projects are similar to those employed for mid-term assessment. According to the company officials interviewed, answers will be sought to such questions as the following:

(a) have the previously specified technical targets been met? If not, what has been the reason?
(b) was the research completed according to plan and within the allocated budget?
(c) has the technology developed been transferred to operating divisions, and, if so, how many cases of transfer have occurred? If not, have the problems been technical, organizational or the result of changed market conditions?
(d) is the technology transferred being commercialized? If so, what is the likely return on investment in terms of (i) sales of new or improved products or processes, and (ii) reduction in production costs?
(e) have any less tangible benefits resulted such as improvement in safety or future product quality?
(f) what impact has the project had on other company technologies? Have any patents resulted, and how important are these likely to prove?
(g) has the project resulted in publications and do these show evidence of high quality research? Is there any work that should be followed up in the future?
(h) has the research produced any other spin-offs (e.g. new techniques) or externalities (e.g. publicity for the company)?

Those interviewed reported that 'rate-of-return' calculations are annually updated for several years after a project's completion and that the basis of these figures is often the subject of debate both within laboratories and with operating divisions who generally pay a proportion of the research costs. Difficulties may arise with calculating economic returns for generic projects with a diffuse impact across several technology areas or product groups. Researchers have added to the problem by often being unduly optimistic about the commercial prospects for projects they are eager to promote. Two companies reported that criticism from operating divisions has resulted in researchers becoming more realistic in their predictions. Although subject to less error than the calculations for strategic research, the degree to which predicted 'rates of return' on investment are in accord with subsequent outcomes is still not very high.

All five companies stressed the centrality of good internal communications as a means of achieving successful technology transfer, and for this reason there is considerable cross-representation on laboratory and operating division committees. In part, this reflects the traditional emphasis in R&D management on consensus-seeking mechanisms which necessarily have to represent the views of all interested parties. A variety of other technology transfer mechanisms are also used — for example, the NEC Central R&D Group holds an annual technology exhibition for operating divisions at which the laboratory's work is marketed and internal research contracts gained.

Finally, mention should be made of the evaluation of researchers. Although companies vary in the stress they place on the assessment of individuals as opposed to teams, all operate formal systems for annual personnel review. Quantitative indicators are normally employed such as numbers of reports, published papers, patents and presentations at industrial research associations and other professional meetings, as well as rankings of researchers according to a variety of criteria (one firm uses a grading system based on twenty separate factors).[4] However, this is always complemented by in-depth qualitative judgements made by more senior laboratory staff. Feedback of the evaluation results is seen as particularly important as is public recognition of success. One company stressed the value of its system of internal awards for scientific and technical success. Ten to twenty prizes are given annually to researchers for work resulting in significant commercial benefits, potentially important inventions, or novel incremental improvements to production technology or products. Decisions on awards are made by a committee drawn from senior corporate and laboratory management.

Evaluation of Government-Funded Research

The companies visited all reported that applied research funded by government is primarily for longer-term work and comes principally from subsidies for participation in the Sunshine, Moonlight, Large-Scale Project and Basic Technology for Future Industries programmes supported by the Agency for Industrial Science and Technology. As noted in Chapter 3, such programmes aim to develop collaborative pre-competitive research at the national level between industry, government institutes and universities in technology areas seen as strategically important for the future. The rationale for company participation was clearly stated by one of the officials interviewed:

We welcome participation in government programmes when we want to build up a new technology area. We do not welcome research projects in areas near our current commercial activities since, among other things, there is patent friction. The important purpose of national collaborative projects is to develop the possibility of future large-scale business opportunities in carefully targeted areas. All interested companies participate in developing the fundamental technology, and, with government participation, this makes the basic research pie much bigger. [5]

Government funding as a proportion of total R&D expenditure varied across companies from one to five per cent, although it was as high as fifteen per cent of the budget of central research laboratories. Firms reported that the grants received for projects in practice cover a maximum of fifty per cent of actual costs, and often as little as twenty per cent. Consequently, decisions to participate are made on grounds similar to those for other longer-term strategic research, so projects have to be in areas prioritized by the company as important for the future. Although dislike was voiced of the bureaucracy involved in submitting proposals and regular reports to government agencies, this was generally more than counterbalanced by the fact that risky projects beyond an individual company's capability could be attempted in an environment of managed technological competition with other firms.[6]

As for evaluation by firms of government-funded research, the procedures employed were reported as being no different in principle to those for other longer-term strategic research described above. Evaluation by AIST of company participation in its programmes was covered in Chapter 3 and therefore requires little further discussion here. Two points should, however, be noted. First, companies felt strongly that it was neither the role nor was it within the capability of government to evaluate rates-of-return on the research projects they support. Evaluation of the commercial benefits of long-term research cannot realistically be undertaken until at least three, and preferably five, years after a project's completion. Instead, assessment by AIST and other agencies should concentrate on the extent to which technical and other strategic goals (for example, building a national capability in a particular technology area) have been achieved.

Second, the officials interviewed felt that 'additionality' (the extent to which state funds generate new research activities which would otherwise not have been undertaken by firms) was an inappropriate criterion to use in evaluation.[7] If a government-supported project progresses satisfactorily, firms will certainly contribute more of their own resources but such additional investment is generally a matter of commercial secrecy and is not something they would wish to divulge. There is also a danger that such an indicator could be manipulated since it is easy for companies to claim that a project would not have gone ahead in the absence of government funding or that subsequent activities are a direct consequence of prior support. In any case, the procedures used to select projects mean that 'additionality' is built into programmes in terms of scale (firms would not otherwise collaborate) and acceleration of research.[8]

Views on Research Evaluation Within Government

The companies interviewed generally welcomed the increasing emphasis given by government to the evaluation of research, and felt in particular that the assessment procedures used in more recent programmes such as Basic Technology for Future Industries were working relatively well. The introduction of systematic mid-term review was seen as an especially important development. Firms do not wish to see more regular monitoring since this would place unnecessary bureaucratic demands on them and impair creativity among the collaborating researchers.

The opinions expressed by firms on research evaluation within government institutes were more mixed. Most felt that, while a few laboratories are fulfilling their missions extremely well (ETL and NIRIM were cited in this respect) and many others are performing adequately, some are not up to standard. Although the situation has been improving slowly, routine research too often continues long after any possible utility has disappeared. It was argued that change is difficult to achieve because of the high proportion of core-funding at some institutes, the system of lifetime employment of staff and associated limitations on mobility, ageing problems, and a traditional emphasis on internal assessment of research performance. The underlying problem was thus seen as systemic, and the policy of funding agencies gradually to increase the proportion of institute activities devoted to collaborative research with industry was therefore supported.

Those interviewed also felt that the Administrative Inspection Bureau was playing a useful role in promoting acceptance of the need for external review of institutes. While more formalized internal review of the type advocated by the Council for Science and

Technology is certainly necessary, firms argued that the most important requirement is for funding agencies to initiate a system for regular external review of their laboratories. In particular, visiting groups should contain a high proportion of industrialists with expert knowledge of relevant research fields. They should also be vested with strong powers for recommending change.

Notes

1. It should be stressed that the firms visited are all large enterprises at the leading-edge of technology in their sectors of activity. Consequently, the conclusions drawn about evaluation in this chapter do not necessarily apply to small and medium-sized firms. Given the current emphasis by AIST and STA on creative basic technology, company participation in government-funded applied programmes is generally limited to larger firms.
2. The use of forecasting and prediction in project selection is a subject that is currently exciting a great deal of interest among research managers and corporate planners in Japan. The methods and techniques employed by Canon and Sumitomo are discussed, respectively, in Yamouchi (1983) and Nagasaki *et al.* (1983). A more general discussion is given in Irvine and Martin (1984).
3. It is important for companies that staff working in key future technology areas retain strong links with the specialist research community in their field, and journal publication and conference attendance are seen as valuable mechanisms for achieving this aim. Companies also reported that significant prestige is attached in Japan to making major technological breakthroughs which are widely discussed in the media. These are exploited in the marketing of both consumer and industrial products, and are seen as giving a guarantee to the public that the company is at the leading-edge and therefore technically trustworthy.
4. The criteria employed for assessing individual researchers normally include psychological factors relating to the extent staff are able to work effectively in harmony with other team members. One firm reported that achieving balance between the individual drive that is often necessary for progress to be made in research, and maintenance of relations with other staff, is regarded as a particularly important issue for R&D management.
5. One company also mentioned that participation in longer-term development programmes — for example, concerning fuel-cell technology in the Moonlight programme — is often necessary to gain authorization from government or public corporations for new products which have to meet official standards set for public purchasing. Another firm stressed that participation in information technology projects can be a useful means of

ensuring that they are not excluded from discussions in which, for example, national standards for operating systems are established.
6. The argument is sometimes made in Western nations that Japanese companies have on occasion been railroaded by MITI into participating in collaborative programmes of little immediate interest. Compliance is necessary because firms do not want to exclude themselves from the ongoing consensus-based processes of establishing national technology policy, and MITI plays a central role in the all-important international trade negotiations. This view was not expressed by any of the companies visited, although no direct questions were posed about the existence of such friction.
7. 'Additionality' is one of the five criteria used by the UK Department of Trade and Industry to evaluate applied research (the others are 'innovativeness', 'technical success', 'degree of exploitation' and 'financial success'). Rankings of each are made on a five-point scale.
8. Probably the most important criticism of the use of 'additionality' in evaluation is its inherent conservatism—the research scoring highest is often by definition work of borderline importance that firms would not have carried out in the absence of state subsidies. The Japanese approach is rather to employ government funding to coordinate and target research of the highest priority which would in any case be carried out by companies.

6
Conclusions

The final task remaining is to summarize the procedures being used to assess government-funded applied research in Japan, and come to an overall view of how well evaluation systems are working in practice. By identifying their strengths and weaknesses, certain lessons can be drawn in relation to improving evaluation activities in the United Kingdom.

Main Features of Japanese Evaluation System

Although differences exist across funding agencies and programmes, several features can be identified as characterizing the Japanese approach to assessing applied research:

(i) The main aim of research evaluation is to assist in the effective management of R&D by contributing to decisions on planning, resource allocation, and the selection (or continuation) of projects or programmes. There has been significant effort among both mission-oriented agencies and firms to improve the research management function, and for this reason the procedures employed for project selection and review have generally been closely integrated. In recent years, however, a second rationale for research evaluation has emerged in that it is increasingly required to demonstrate that R&D programmes have produced benefits justifying their cost. In particular, the political demand to ensure government expenditures are utilized efficiently is leading to greater stress on external auditing of research performance, with the Administrative Inspection Bureau playing a major role in developing a central government capacity in this respect.

(ii) It is accepted best practice that evaluation objectives are set at the outset of a project and are actually built into the R&D plan. A detailed mission definition is a prerequisite to evaluation of any sort — that is, it is necessary to understand the aim of the research, the reason why it is being undertaken, for whom, how the results are intended to be used, and what would constitute success or failure. The Japanese have taken steps to specify clearly the research roles of industrially oriented government laboratories and programmes (primarily to promote the development and diffusion of innovative new technologies), and 'mission relevance' is now a principal criterion in the assessment schedule used by the Administrative Inspection Bureau to evaluate research institutes. The Council for Science and Technology *Guidelines for Research Evaluation* also expressly state that evaluation objectives should be specified clearly in research proposals and plans. Finally, through their participation in joint programmes with institutes, companies appear to have succeeded in exercising a positive influence on the way in which government evaluates research, introducing stricter procedures for setting technical targets where the nature of the R&D allows. The objectives for strategic research must necessarily be framed in more general terms than those for specific applied research where the basic science is normally already in place.

(iii) It is also standard practice that an evaluation plan is agreed at the outset of research. This sets out specified procedures for pre-assessment, mid-term and ex-post assessment, as well as for routine monitoring of research in progress. Use is sometimes made of evaluation flowcharts of the sort outlined in Figure 3 in Chapter 2. Special efforts have been made in recent years to introduce procedures for effective mid-term review, particularly in longer-running programmes, since this enables research goals to be revised in the light of changes in technology or the commercial environment.

(iv) The question of organization and responsibility for evaluation has been a central issue in recent initiatives to improve the procedures and approaches employed. On the one hand, government has emphasized the importance of external evaluation through strengthening the activities of the Administrative Inspection Bureau and requiring all agencies to review their laboratories by the end of 1989. On the other, laboratories are being encouraged to formalize their in-house assessment activities and to take into account the views of 'third-parties'. The relationship between evaluators, the funding body and the researcher can thus take different forms, although greatest reliance is still placed on what is basically self-assessment. A distinctive feature is that little or no use is currently made in Japan of professional evaluators from consultancy companies or institutes, whose activities have been burgeoning in most Western countries. Rather, there is a preference for traditional consensus-seeking evaluation based on committees, which draw upon knowledgeable experts from institutes, universities and industry. The results of evaluations are circulated primarily within funding agencies, although there has been a trend towards more open publication. Prior to this, there is a lengthy consultation process in which those evaluated are given full opportunity to comment on and respond to recommendations.

(v) Finally, it should be noted that recent Japanese attempts to introduce more effective assessment have given priority to the evaluation process itself. Traditional cultural values militate against acceptance of external evaluation, especially if the results are made public, and for this reason care has had to be taken with generating a commitment among researchers that a strengthening of assessment procedures will not only improve efficiency but is also in their own interests. To some extent, the Asahi Research Centre survey (described in Chapter 2) can be seen as an attempt to develop such consensus by seeking the views of large numbers of research managers and scientists. This is reflected in their recommendations that, to be effective, evaluation must be based on a 'common understanding' of its purpose, adequate feedback should be given to researchers, and the assessment criteria must be both appropriate and 'transparent'.

Evaluation Methods and Techniques Employed

A detailed summary of the extent to which specific evaluation methods and techniques are used in the various government agencies and programmes covered in the study is given in Table 7. This illustrates well the general approach to evaluation employed in Japan:

(i) Significant effort is put into ex-ante evaluation (preassessment), with studies often being undertaken into the potential technological or economic importance of particular research fields or programmes. This is complemented in many government

Table 7 Evaluation methods and techniques used to assess applied research in Japan

Organization	Ex-ante studies	Ex-post studies		Quantitative indicators					Internal peer-review			External peer-review			Formal committee review		Personnel review	Customer/'user' review		Others	
	Likely techno-economic impact	Techno-economic impact	Cost-benefit analyses	Publications	Citations or bibliometric analyses	Patents	Technology sales and royalties	Other impact indicators	Project proposal or renewal	Mid-term	Ex-post	Project proposal or renewal	Mid-term	Ex-post	Mid-term	Ex-post	Researcher rating or evaluation	Ex-ante	Ex-post	Formal management systems	Central government research audit
1. Administrative Inspection Bureau		X						X						X							X
2. Agency of Industrial Science and Technology																					
Basic Technologies for Future Industries Programme	X			X		X									X	X		X			
Large-Scale R&D Programme		X		X		X	X								X	X		X		X	
AIST Laboratories	X			X		X	X	X	X						X	X				X	
3. Science and Technology Agency																					
Special Co-ordination Funds	X			X		X			X						X			X		X	
Exploratory Research for Advanced Technology	X			X	X		X	X													
STA Laboratories	X			X		X	X										X	X		X	
Special Corporations (RIKEN)	X			X		X	X	X	X		X			X	X	X	X	X	X	X	
4. Companies	X	X	X	X		X		X	X						X	X	X	X	X	X	X

programmes with 'customer review' in which prospective users of the results are consulted about the utility of new projects or programmes (or indeed directly participate in the planning process).
(ii) Stress has traditionally been laid on routine monitoring of research, with decisions on continuation of funding for projects being made during the annual round of budgetary discussions. In laboratories, this is often undertaken in parallel with yearly reviews of the performance of researchers.
(iii) Over the last few years, routine monitoring of research programmes has increasingly been complemented by the adoption of more formal mid-term and ex-post evaluation. This is normally undertaken by an external review committee whose members are appointed at the outset of a programme and serve until its completion. Conventional peer-review procedures of the sort widely used in Western countries (with programme officers circulating reports for comment to anonymous peers) have to date rarely been used.
(iv) Significant reliance is placed in evaluation on the extent to which pre-established technical targets have been achieved, particularly where specific applied research is concerned. Targets are normally arrived at through lengthy consensus-seeking discussions between companies, laboratories and funding agencies. A 'formal management system' is then set up to check periodically whether planned targets are being met. Because research is usually initiated in the context of agreed industrial or technological objectives, evaluation can in many cases be confined to appraisal of technical performance. The role of agency officials responsible for individual projects is extremely important in managing this process.
(v) Widespread use is made of quantitative indicators in monitoring and assessing research. Publications and patents are utilized as indicators of research output and technological impact, especially in evaluating the contributions made by institutes to longer-term strategic research projects carried out collaboratively with industry. Use is also made of other output indicators (such as numbers of consultants or cases of technology transfer) and data on technology sales or patent royalties. Citation analysis is, however, rarely employed, in part because most relevant research is published in Japanese-language journals which are not scanned by the *Science Citation Index*.
(vi) It has previously not been common for government agencies and laboratories to carry out systematic ex-post studies of the technical

or economic impact of research. More emphasis is, however, now being placed on this, most notably in the audits of research institutes carried out by the Administrative Inspection Bureau, but also in the two AIST applied research programmes (Basic Technology for Future Industries and the Large-Scale R&D Programme). Government does not see it as necessary or feasible to use cost–benefit analysis to estimate the return on its investment in R&D, preferring to evaluate research in terms of its contribution to realizing national strategic technological aims.

(vii) Companies have generally employed a far wider range of evaluation techniques than have government agencies, especially in relation to assessing technological impact and economic return on investment. Cost–benefit analysis is also often used in ex-ante project appraisal.

As for problems experienced in carrying out evaluations, the main difficulties reported concerned strategic applied research where the outputs are diffuse, often long term, and therefore difficult to measure. In many cases, it is not possible to rely on the standard procedure of setting detailed technical targets in advance and then monitoring progress in meeting them. Nor is more systematic mid-term review necessarily the solution since experts on committees may be unduly conservative in their judgements (this was identified in Chapter 4 as the main reason behind failure to agree on an evaluation procedure within the ERATO programme). Consequently, both government and industry are actively seeking to develop better evaluation methods for managing progress in novel basic technological projects and programmes which accord researchers sufficient freedom for creative work while at the same time setting acceptable limits on technical risk. As for evaluating ex-post the impact of such research, there is little option, in the absence of better alternatives, than to rely on the views of experts in the field coupled with publication, patent and technological royalty indicators. Industry in particular has met major problems in applying rate-of-return and other quantitative techniques to assessing longer-term research.

Lessons from Japan

Let us turn finally to the main lessons that can be learned from this study of Japan. The first concerns the extent to which the Japanese are

Conclusions 89

striving to tackle problems similar to those being faced in other industrial countries, especially in relation to the 'mission relevance' and research performance of government institutes. There are close parallels with Britain as regards the difficulties being encountered with staff ageing and renewing old lines of research. Furthermore, in both countries there are inadequate mechanisms for regularly reviewing the research activities of laboratories, a problem which Japanese industry regards as particularly pressing.

Second, much can be learned from the research audits of government laboratories being carried out by the Administrative Inspection Bureau. This is the first time that systematic external review of institutes has been undertaken in Japan, and it appears to be complementing well the attempts being made to increase the level of formal research assessment within both laboratories and the agencies responsible for their funding. Of special note is the reliance placed by AIB on 'hearings' with industry to assess the technological impact and continuing 'mission relevance' of institutes, as well as the use of quantitative techniques in the evaluation process. It is recommended that consideration be given to exploring the extent to which the AIB approach to research assessment might usefully be adopted in the UK context.

The third lesson concerns the need to complement the externally imposed structure of central government evaluation with positive assistance to funding agencies and laboratories with developing the capacity to undertake assessments in-house. Building up evaluation skills is by no means easy, and for this reason the activities of the CST 'Committee on Guidelines for Research Evaluation' in promoting the introduction of R&D assessment techniques are extremely important. Of particular value are the specifications for an effective evaluation system developed by the Committee, and the recommended procedures for monitoring and assessing research performance. These could well be relevant in the UK and would repay further study, as would the background reports commissioned by the Committee from the Asahi Research Centre. It is recommended that the published reports of the Committee be translated into English.

Fourth, certain lessons can be drawn from the experience with introducing more systematic assessment procedures in Japan. Although the trend to increased evaluation of government-funded research was widely welcomed by those interviewed, several potential problems have become apparent:

(a) While the traditional consensus-seeking approach to research management is highly effective in that the findings of evaluations are generally acted upon in full, the need to establish agreement can result in lengthy delays. Moreover, the inherent conservatism in the system can result in an environment which is not conducive to longer-term applied research aiming to produce creative new basic technology.
(b) Research creativity can be impaired if evaluation is carried out too mechanistically (researchers can, for example, learn to maximize their visibility in terms of specified output indicators but at the expense of innovative work).
(c) Undue pressure to demonstrate immediate technological output may stifle longer-term research where the commercial impact is often diffuse and only becomes evident several years later. The timing of post-hoc evaluation therefore needs to take into account the nature of the research being assessed.
(d) There is a temptation for government to adopt evaluation techniques which lend themselves to simple quantification — for example, while rate-of-return techniques may be appropriate for R&D within individual companies, they were widely felt to be unsuitable for government-funded research.
(e) The commercial significance of many joint industry-institute research programmes means that the issue of industrial involvement in project selection and evaluation is sometimes problematic and needs to be handled sensitively. However, given the stress on technical appraisal in the evaluation process, Japanese industry seems willing to accept the use by agencies of disinterested experts from universities and laboratories on assessment committees for applied research programmes.

Finally, if there is one all-important lesson to be drawn from Japan, it is the benefits that flow from achieving close integration of the planning, management, monitoring and evaluation of research. This is nowhere better demonstrated than in the 'Basic Technology for Future Industries' programme where mid-term assessment is tied to the task of concentrating resources on the most promising lines of work as projects unfold and the research becomes progressively more applied. Moreover, the long consensus-seeking process of project definition in which verifiable aims are agreed by research institutes, companies and government, means that evaluation can usually be focused on technical outcomes. The relevance and technological importance of the research are planned in from the beginning, as are the mechanisms for technology transfer and implementation. In short, evaluation should, wherever possible, be built into the management of applied research before a project begins. It should not just be added on at the end for auditing purposes as often happens in the United Kingdom and most other Western nations.

References

Agency of Industrial Science and Technology (1986a), *AIST 1986*, Tokyo: MITI.
Agency of Industrial Science and Technology (1986b), *National Research and Development Program (Large-Scale Project)*, Tokyo: MITI.
Agency of Industrial Science and Technology (1987), *Research and Development Project of Basic Technology for Future Industries*, Tokyo: MITI.
Agency of Industrial Science and Technology (nd), *National Chemical Laboratory for Industry*, Tokyo: MITI.
Asahi Research Centre (1982), *Review of Methods of Research Evaluation, Vol. 1 (Summary), Vol. 2 (Main Report) and Appendix (Results of Survey)*, Report to Science and Technology Agency, Tokyo.
Asahi Research Centre (1983), *Review of Methods of Research Evaluation: Current Situation of Research Evaluation Abroad and in the Japanese Private Sector*, Report to Science and Technology Agency, Tokyo.
Asahi Research Centre (1984), *Review of Methods of Research Evaluation*, Report to Science and Technology Agency, Tokyo.
Cabinet Office (1986), *Annual Review of Government-Funded R&D 1986*, London: HMSO.
Council for Science and Technology (1984), *Overall Basic Policy for Promotion of Science and Technology in Long-Range Perspective to Cope with Recent Changes in Circumstances*, Tokyo: CST.
Council for Science and Technology, Policy Committee, Prime Minister's Office, and Committee on Guidelines for Research Evaluation (1986a), *Basic View on Research Evaluation*, Tokyo: CST.
Council for Science and Technology, Policy Committee, Prime Minister's Office, and Committee on Guidelines for Research Evaluation (1986b), *Guidelines for Research Evaluation*, Tokyo: CST.
Council for Science and Technology (1986c), 'And the Next . . .', document outlining Special Co-ordination Funds for Science and Technology, Tokyo: CST.
Electrotechnical Laboratory (1986), 'Draft Management Review Report', mimeo, Tsukuba: ETL.
Frieman, W. (1987), 'Beyond Translation: Using Technical Literature for Competitive Assessments', mimeo: Science Applications International Corporation, USA.

Gibbons, M. and Georghiou, L. (1987), 'Evaluation of Applied Research—A Report to the UK Department of Trade and Industry', mimeo, London: DTI.
Industrial Technology Council, Sub-Committee on Assessment (1986), *Final Assessment Report on the R&D Project on Optical Measurement Control Systems*, Tokyo: MITI.
Institute of Physical and Chemical Research (1986), *Frontier Research Programme*, Saitama: RIKEN.
Irvine, J. and Martin, B.R. (1984), *Foresight in Science: Picking the Winners*, London and New York: Frances Pinter.
Irvine, J. and Martin, B.R. (1986), *British Science Evaluation Methods*, Science Policy Study—Hearings Volume 13, Task Force on Science Policy of the Committee on Science and Technology, House of Representatives, Ninety-Ninth Congress, First Session, 30 October 1985, Washington, DC: US Government Printing Office.
JRDC (1986), *Research Development Corporation of Japan*, Tokyo: JRDC.
Kataoka, S. (1986a), 'Three-Dimensional ICs for an Artificial Retina', *IEEE Electrotechnology Review*, pp. 46–7.
Kataoka, S. (1986b), 'Three-Dimensional Integrated Sensors', paper presented at 'IEDM 1986', mimeo, Tenri: Sharp Corporation.
Kodama, F., Nishioka, S., Osada, H., and Kurita, M. (1981), 'Possibilities for Establishing a Research Evaluation System in Japan: Analysis of National Research Institutions', Report to Science and Technology Agency, mimeo, Tokyo: Asahi Research Centre.
Kurachi, S. (nd), 'A New Approach to the Development of Radically New Technologies', mimeo, Tokyo: Research Development Corporation of Japan.
Logsdon, J.M. and Rubin, C.B. (1985), *An Overview of Federal Research Evaluation Activities*, Report to National Science Foundation (PRA–8400686), Washington, DC: The George Washington University.
Luukkonen-Gronow, T. (1987), 'Scientific Research Evaluation: A Review of Various Methods and their Contexts of Application', *R&D Management* 17 (3), pp. 207–22.
Lynn, L. (1986), 'Japanese Research and Technology Policy', *Science*, Vol. 233, pp. 296–301.
Management and Co-ordination Agency (1984), *Current Framework for Administrative Reform*, Tokyo: MCA, 25 January.
Management and Co-ordination Agency (1985), *Management and Co-ordination Agency: Organization and Functions*, Tokyo: MCA.
Management and Co-ordination Agency, Administrative Inspection Bureau (1986), *Report on the Survey of Special Corporations*, Tokyo: MCA.
Martin B.R., Irvine, J., Narin, F. and Sterritt, C. (1987), 'The Continuing Decline in British Science', *Nature*, Vol. 330, pp. 123–6.
Nagasaki, S., Motoyoshi, K. and Okano, K. (1983), 'Research Evaluation in Sumitomo Electric Industry', *Communications of the Operational Research*

Society of Japan, Vol. 28 (2), pp. 533–9.
Nagasu, H. (1983), 'The Evaluation of R&D Programmes in Japan – The Case of the National Aerospace Laboratory', paper presented at European Commission Seminar on the Evaluation of Research and Development, Brussels, 17–18 October, mimeo, Directorate-General for Science, Research and Development, Commission of the European Communities.
NIRIM (1986), *National Institute for Research in Inorganic Materials, 1986*, Tsukuba: NIRIM.
National Research Institute for Metals (nd), 'Technical Targets of Jisedai Project and Results Obtained in Designed Alloys', mimeo, Tokyo: NRIM.
NRIM (1985), *National Institute for Metals, 1985–86*, Tokyo: NRIM.
OECD (1987), *Evaluation of Research: A Selection of Current Practices*, Paris: Organization for Economic Cooperation and Development.
Office of Technology Assessment (1986), *Research Funding as an Investment: Can We Measure the Returns?*, Washington, DC: US Congress Office of Technology Assessment (OTA-TM-SET 36).
Ormala, E. (1987), *Evaluation of Technical Research – Experience of Practices and Methods in the Nordic Countries*, Helsinki: Nordic Co-operative Organization for Applied Research (NORDFORSK).
Research Development Corporation of Japan (1986), *ERATO: Exploratory Research for Advanced Technology*, Tokyo: JRDC.
Research and Development Institute of Metals and Composites for Future Industries (1984), *New Materials: Metals and Composites*, Tokyo: IMCFI.
Science and Technology Agency (1985a), *White Paper on Science and Technology 1985 – New Development of R&D and the Era of Cooperation (Summary)*, Tokyo: STA (English language translation by Foreign Press Centre).
Science and Technology Agency (1985b), *STA – Its Roles and Activities 1985*, Tokyo: STA.
Shibata, M. (1987), 'Research Evaluation in RIKEN', mimeo, Saitama: Institute of Physical and Chemical Research.
Statistics Bureau, Management and Co-ordination Agency (1987), *Report on the Survey of Research and Development, 1986*, Tokyo: Management and Co-ordination Agency, Prime Minister's Office.
Stokes, D.E. (1982), 'Perceptions of the Nature of Basic and Applied Science in the United States', in A. Gerstenfeld (Ed.), *Science Policy Perspectives: USA – Japan*, New York: Academic Press.
Tanaka, M. (1987), 'Evaluation of Innovation Policies in Japan' (draft), mimeo: Graduate School for Policy Science, Saitama University.
Tanaka, S. *et al.* (1985), *Final Assessment on Fortified ICs for Extreme Conditions*, Report of Assessment Committee, Research and Development Project of Basic Technology for Future Industries, Tokyo: MITI/AIST.
Yamauchi, I. (1983), 'Long Range Strategic Planning in Japanese R&D', paper presented at International Seminar on Innovation, Design and Long Cycles in Economic Development, Royal College of Art, London, 13–15 April,

mimeo, Kajiwara: Nomura Research Institute.

Yamouchi, T. (1983), 'Project Evaluation in Canon, Inc.', *Communications of the Operational Research Society of Japan*, Vol. 28 (2), pp. 540–5.

Yoshimura, H. (1987), 'The Organization of Science and Technology in Japan', paper presented at International Conference on the Organization of Science and Technology in Western Industrialized Countries — An International Comparison, Bonn, 26–7 May.

Appendix 1
List of Officials Consulted

Mr G. Chiba, Director, ERATO Programme, Research Development Corporation of Japan, 2-5-2 Nagata-cho, Chiyoda-ku, Tokyo 100.

Dr. O. Hayama, Executive Director, Industrial Department, Nomura Research Institute, 4-7-1 Kajiwara, Kamakura, Kanagawa.

Mr H. Hosoda, Deputy Director, Coordination Division, Science and Technology Policy Bureau, Science and Technology Agency, 2-2-1 Kasumigaseki, Chiyoda-ku, Tokyo.

Dr Z. Inoue, Senior Researcher and Head, Planning Section, National Institute for Research in Inorganic Materials, Namiki 1-1, Sakura-mura, Nihari-gun, Ibaraki-ken 305.

Mr Y. Kanazawa, Senior Staff Member, Planning Division, Science and Technology Policy Bureau, Science and Technology Agency, 2-2-1 Kasumigaseki, Chiyoda-ku, Tokyo.

Dr S. Kataoka, Corporate Director, Group Deputy General Manager, Engineering Centre, Divisional General Manager, Central Research Laboratories, Sharp Corporation, 2613-1 Ichinomoto-cho, Tenri-shi, Nara 632.

Dr K. Kishida, Director, General Manager, R&D Planning and Administration Department, Mitsubishi Electric Corporation, 2-3 Marunouchi 2-chome, Chiyoda-ku, Tokyo 100.

Professor F. Kodama, Graduate School for Policy Science, Saitama University, 255 Shimo Okubo, Urawa-shi 338, Saitama.

Mr Y. Kurita, Senior Officer for Research Planning, National Research Laboratory of Metrology, Agency of Industrial Science and Technology, 1-1-4 Umezono, Sakura-mura, Nihari, Ibaraki 305.

Mr N. Motoshima, Deputy Director, Technology Research and Information Division, Agency of Industrial Science and Technology, Ministry of International Trade and Industry, 1-3-1 Kasumigaseki, Chiyoda-ku, Tokyo.

Dr E. Nakano, Director, Research Planning Office, Mechanical Engineering Laboratory, Agency of Industrial Science and Technology, 1-2 Namiki, Tsukuba Science City, Ibaraki-ken 305.

Appendix 1 97

Mr O. Nishiyama, Deputy Director, Office of Basic Technology for Future Industries, Agency of Industrial Science and Technology, Ministry of International Trade and Industry, 1-3-1 Kasumigaseki, Chiyoda-ku, Tokyo.

Dr I. Ogata, Director General, National Chemical Laboratory for Industry, Ministry of International Trade and Industry, Yatabe, Ibaraki 305.

Mr T. Ohashi, Inspector, Administrative Inspection Bureau, Management and Coordination Agency, Office of the Prime Minister, Godochosa No. 4 go-kan, 3-1-1- Kasumigaseki, Chiyoda-ku, Tokyo 100.

Mr K. Ohtaki, Senior Assistant Director, Large-Scale R&D Project Office, Agency of Industrial Science and Technology, Ministry of International Trade and Industry, 1-3-1 Kasumigaseki, Chiyoda-ku, Tokyo.

Dr A. Shaku, Deputy Director-General, National Research Institute for Metals, 2-3-12 Nakameguro, Meguroku, Tokyo 153.

Mr M. Shibata, Director for International Cooperation, The Institute of Physical and Chemical Research (RIKEN), 2-1 Wako-shi, Saitama 351-01.

Mr K. Tamura, Head, Planning Section, Electrotechnical Laboratory, Agency of Industrial Science and Technology, 1-1-4 Umezono, Sakura-mura, Nihari-gun, Ibaraki 305.

Mr K. Tamura, Assistant Manager, International Programmes Planning Office, Japan Information Centre for Science and Technology (JICST), 5-2 Nagato-cho 2-chome, Chiyoda-ku, Tokyo 100.

Dr M. Uchida, General Manager, Research and Development Promotion Centre, Corporate Research and Technology Coordination Department, Hitachi Ltd., New Marunouchi Building, 5-1 Marunouchi 1-chome, Chiyoda-ku, Tokyo.

Dr T. Uchida, Associate Senior Vice President and Director, NEC Corporation, 1-1 Miyazaki 4-chome, Miyamae-ku, Kawasaki, Kanagawa 213.

Dr N. Ueda, Assistant General Manager, R&D Planning Department, Toray Industries Inc., 2 Nihonbashi-Muromachi 2-chome, Chuo-ku, Tokyo 103.

Appendix 2
Sample Questionnaire for Visit to Science and Technology Agency Affiliated Laboratories (NRIM, NIRIM and RIKEN)

Aim of Visit

The reason for the visit is to learn about the experience of Japanese government laboratories in evaluating the success and impact of their applied research programmes. The term applied research is defined here as:

original investigation undertaken in order to acquire new knowledge which is directed towards practical aims or objectives. Some applied research is *strategic* where practical applications are likely and feasible but cannot yet be clearly specified. *Specific* applied research has as its aim a quite specific and detailed product, process, system etc.

Through this study of Japanese approaches to research evaluation, the British Department of Trade and Industry hopes to learn some lessons which may be of value in improving the effectiveness and value for money of the applied research programmes it supports, especially in its own laboratories.

Questions

1. In general, what ex-post evaluation is undertaken of the success of applied research carried out in the laboratory?
2. At what level do you carry out such evaluation? Do you evaluate:
   (a) the research of individual scientists or project teams?
   (b) the success of specific projects or programmes?
   (c) the success of the laboratory as a whole?

3. What is normally the aim of research evaluation in your laboratory? Is it, for example, to provide background information for future funding decisions, to assess the extent to which the work has contributed to technical progress or to evaluate the performance of researchers?
4. Who is responsible for undertaking research evaluation? Is it done in-house or does STA carry it out centrally? Who initiates evaluations, how often are they undertaken and what happens to completed studies? What is the relationship between the evaluators, the researchers, laboratory management and STA?
5. What criteria are used to choose the new applied research programmes and projects started in your laboratory?
6. What criteria are used to judge the success of completed research in your laboratory? How are they related to those used to select new projects? Does the laboratory generally find it helpful to require verifiable detailed objectives for applied research before it is undertaken?
7. What methods and techniques (e.g. peer review, policy committee review) are used in your laboratory to evaluate the success and impact of applied research? To what extent are quantitative measures used — e.g. numbers of publications and citations, patents, benefits gained by industry etc?
8. One of the main aims of the applied research carried out in your laboratory is to produce useful new knowledge for Japanese industry and government agencies. How do you assess whether the research is of any benefit? What measures do you or would you use to judge commercial and technological impact?
9. At what stage in a research project or programme is evaluation normally conducted? Is it carried out only after the project has finished or is evaluation built into the research from the outset? Is there usually any mid-term review of research projects or programmes?
10. What is the nature of your regular monitoring of programmes? How is this undertaken and what parties are involved? How does regular monitoring relate to other review activities and ex-post evaluation?
11. What mechanisms are used to feed back the results of evaluations to researchers? When is this done?
12. What has been the experience in the laboratory with the use of particular evaluation techniques? Are there any approaches to evaluation that you would especially recommend?

13. Are there any other laboratories you are familiar with that employ systematic approaches to evaluation of research and from which I might learn some useful lessons?
14. Could we possibly discuss in detail three major programmes of applied research carried out in your laboratory, focusing on one that was completed perhaps two years ago and was successful, one that was also completed two years ago but was not so successful, and one that is currently nearing completion. I would like to know for each:

    (a) the reason why it was originally funded — what expectations were there of the research?
    (b) the criteria that were used/are being used to judge the success of the research?
    (c) whether detailed verifiable objectives for the research were set up before it was begun?
    (d) the techniques used to evaluate the research, especially where quantitative measures were/are being employed?
    (e) how it is possible to assess whether the research is of benefit to industry or to government agencies?
    (f) at what stage in the research was evaluation carried out?
    (g) whether the evaluation produced any useful information that could help the researchers involved improve their performance on future projects, and how such feedback is given to staff?
    (h) who carried out the evaluation, and what types of information, skills and experiences were necessary?
    (i) whether there were any lessons learned about the strengths and weaknesses of the evaluation techniques used?

15. Finally, does the laboratory feel that the current level and nature of research evaluation is satisfactory? Are there any plans to make changes in evaluation activities by either the laboratory or by STA?

Index

Administrative Inspection Bureau (AIB) xii–xiv, 3, 4, 11–20, 31, 80, 83–4, 88, 89
   case-studies of inspection 17–20
   Division for Comprehensive Survey of Administrative Institutions and Corporations 14
   inspection of research activities 14–15
   Management and Coordination Agency (MCA) 3, 12, 14
Agency of Industrial Science and Technology (AIST) xiv, 3, 4, 10, 15, 31, 34–57, 58, 69, 78, 79–80, 81
   C1 Chemical Technology Project 45–8
   Industrial Technology Council 38–9, 44, 48
   Key Technology Centre 50
   'Moonlight' Programme 10, 78, 81
   'Sunshine' Programme 10, 78
   see also evaluation committees
Asahi Research Centre (ARC) xiii, 21
Asahi Report on Research Evaluation in Japan 21–4, 85, 89

Basic Technology for Future Industries Programme xiv, 3, 53, 67, 69, 71, 78, 80, 88, 90
   case-study of evaluation 41–3
   evaluation of programme 39–41
   outline of programme 34–9
   see also evaluation committees

Chiba, Genya 66–8
citations, as a performance indicator xiv, 19, 66, 71, 87

collaborative research xiv, xv, xvi, 11, 38, 52–3, 78–9, 82, 90
   international collaboration 58
commercial influences xiv, 84
benefits from R & D xii, xv, xvi, 1, 79, 83, 88, 90
Committee on Guidelines for Research Evaluation xiii, 4, 11–12, 20–32, 55–6, 61, 66, 84, 89 see also Council for Science and Technology
committees, evaluation see evaluation committees
consultants xii
   evaluation by 85
   see also Asahi Research Centre
Council for Science and Technology (CST) xiii, 3, 4, 11–12, 32, 33, 58, 80–1
   classification of research 7, 27–8
   1984 Report on 11th Inquiry of the CST 8–9
   Subcommittee on Basic Research 61
   Subcommittee on Research Evaluation 20, 61–2
   Subcommittee on Research Survey 61
   see also Committee on Guidelines for Research Evaluation
culture, Japanese vs Western xvi, 24, 55, 85

ERATO programme 3, 58, 71, 72
   evaluation of programme 64–8, 88
   Fine Polymer Project 68
   outline of programme 63–4
   Perfect Crystal Project 68
   Ultra-Fine Particle Project 68

102 Index

Electrotechnical Laboratory (ETL) 3, 11, 34, 49–50, 53, 57, 70, 80
evaluation committees xiv, xv, 11, 72, 87
 AIST committees 38–49
 company committees 76
 CST committees 61–2
 STA committees 70–1, 72
Exploratory Research for Advanced Technology Programme *see* ERATO Programme

Guidelines for research evaluation *see* Committee on Guidelines for Research Evaluation

Hitachi Ltd 3, 49
 evaluation of research 73–81

Institute for Future Technology 66
Institute of Physical and Chemical Research (RIKEN) 3, 15, 17–18, 32, 58, 68–9
 Council of Laboratory Directors (CLD) 70–1
 procedures for evaluation 69–71

JRDC *see* Research Development Corporation of Japan
Japan, administrative structure of science and technology 4–6
 Ministry of Finance 66
 organization of government 13
Japan Association for the Promotion of the Electronic Industry 41–2
Japan Atomic Energy Research Institute 15
Japan Industrial Technology Association (JITA) 56
Japan Information Centre for Science and Technology 3, 15
Jisedai Project on Advanced Alloys with Controlled Crystalline Structures 40–1

Kataoka, Dr S 41–3
Kondo, Dr J 20–1
Kurachi, Shogo 63–4

language, Japanese 1
 need for English translation of reports xiii, 33, 89
 problems for citation analysis 87
Large-Scale R & D Programme 3, 34, 56, 78, 88
 case-study of programme 49–50
 outline of programme 44–5
 procedures for evaluation 45–9

Mechanical Engineering Laboratory (MEL) 3, 34, 50–6
Ministry of International Trade and Industry (MITI) *see* Agency for Industrial Science and Technology
Mitsubishi Electric Corporation 4
 evaluation of research 73–81

NEC Corporation 4
 evaluation of research 73–81
Nakasone, Prime Minister 9
National Aerospace Laboratory (NAL) 57, 68
National Chemical Laboratory for Industry (NCLI) 3, 15, 34, 50–1
National Institute for Research in Inorganic Materials (NIRIM) 3, 58, 68–9, 72, 80
 procedures for evaluation 69–71
National Research Institute for Metals (NRIM) 3, 58, 68–9
 procedures for evaluation 69–71
National Research Laboratory of Metrology (NRLM) 3, 15, 18–19, 34, 50–1, 53–5
National Space Development Agency (NASDA) 68
Nomura Research Institute 4

Office for Large-Scale R & D Projects *see* Large-Scale R & D Programme
Office for R & D of Basic Technology for Future Industries *see* Basic Technology for Future Industries Programme

Index 103

patents, as a performance indicator xiv, xv, 19, 41, 43, 49, 50, 55, 62, 67–8, 69, 70, 75, 76, 78, 79, 87, 88
peer-review xiv, 8, 24, 55, 70, 87
Prime Minister's Office 3, 8, 12
Project on Three Dimensional ICs 41–3
publications, as a performance indicator xiv, xv, 18, 19, 41, 43, 49, 50, 54–5, 62, 67, 69, 71, 74–5, 76, 78, 81, 87, 88

Research and Development Association for Future Electronic Devices 42
Research Development Corporation of Japan (JRDC) 3, 56, 63–6, 72
see also ERATO Programme
research staff, attitude to assessment 22
average age 11
performance assessment xv, 3, 19, 78, 81, 87
stifling of creativity xvi, 43, 80, 88, 90
see also patents and publications
review committees see evaluation committees
RIKEN see Institute of Physical and Chemical Research

Saitama University, Graduate School for Policy Science 4
Science Citation Index 87
Science Council of Japan 21
Science and Technology Agency (STA) xiii, 2, 3, 4, 10, 18, 21, 31, 58–72, 81

Science and Technology Policy Bureau 3
Sharp Corporation 4
Central Research Laboratories 41
evaluation of research 73–81
Social Development Research Institute 15
Special Co-ordination Funds for Science and Technology Programme 31, 58, 69
approach to evaluation 61–3
outline of programme 61
Sumitomo Ltd 49

Toray Industries 4
evaluation of research 73–81
Tsukuba Science City 53

United Kingdom, Cabinet Office Science and Technology Assessment Office 12
Cabinet Office/Treasury Joint Management Unit 12
Department of Trade and Industry xv, 1, 4; Assessment Unit 4; evaluation criteria for research xv, 82
lessons from Japan xii, xiii, xvi, 1, 4, 72, 83, 88–91
National Audit Office 12

White Paper on Science and Technology 1985 11